Praise for *Overcoming Toxic Emotions*

"Leah Guy writes from experience. She has been through the fire, and transformed that experience into lights of truth. Read her, experience her, and be illumined by all she has to share."

—Michael Fitzpatrick, recipient of The Prince Charles Award for Musical Excellence conferred by HRH the Prince of Wales

"Leah is a gifted writer, healer, and teacher. This book is next level for anyone who wants to grow in their personal and spiritual life. It's a book we all need right now to elevate the consciousness and vibration of ourselves and the world. Leah is a trusted resource and I applaud her journey."

—Suleman Shah, owner of Namaste Bookshop

"I want the reader to know that this is one of the most remarkable books I've read in years on self-help and awakening. My personal library contains over eight thousand books, and I spent over eight years in my early career sharing an office with a fabulous clinical psychologist, Dr. Harold Hansen. I can tell you that Leah Guy's book is one of the finest, offering substantial and meaningful self-help and guidance. She carries us through in brilliantly written pages as to how we can change our energy, and relate more effectively with others. I was impressed when she communicated a value that has rarely been messaged today . . . and that is, walking in someone else's shoes."

—The Amazing Kreskin, world-renowned mentalist

"*Overcoming Toxic Emotions* is a must-read for anyone wanting to have healthier and happier relationships. The three-step method Leah provides is a powerful tool that can be applied to any aspect of your life. Once you master this simple and practical method, you realize healing and transformation are possible. Take yourself on this exciting journey!"

—Christy Whitman, *New York Times* bestselling author of *The Art of Having It All*

"In *Overcoming Toxic Emotions*, author Leah Guy takes a deep dive into what toxic emotions are, and how they hold us back from experiencing joy and fulfillment. She provides a clear and well-articulated road map to freedom from these emotions, and to a more satisfying, self-directed life. This book can help many."

—Chris Kilham, medicine hunter

"Leah Guy is an authentic mind/body/spirit healer par excellence. With a wide-open heart she leads people, teaches people, heals people, and learns from people. Leah's list of followers continues to grow daily as people hear of her work. I am one of them."

—Cynthia D. Chase, author of *From Stressed to Blessed*

"Emotions are contagious, for better or worse. When we are in the grip of toxic emotions, we suffer, and we usually spread suffering. What if you could learn to free yourself from these negative patterns so you could enjoy more happiness and enrich all your relationships? In this compelling work, Leah Guy shares her deep insight into how you can become aware of and then transcend maladaptive habits of body and mind. Essential reading for all who are ready to move beyond negative conditioning and make life more beautiful by creating loving and healthy relationships with themselves and others. Highly recommend."

—Michael J. Gelb, author of *How to Think Like Leonardo da Vinci* and *The Art of Connection*

"Leah Guy has assessed the difficult situation into which so many of us were born, tracked those imprints into our reality today, and in this thoughtful and practical book, provides tools and perspectives through which we can really do something about self-healing. In short, we can take our lives back, evolve our mind-body frequency to another level, and take a deeper dive into our human potential. Thanks, Leah. for being such a good guide."

—Mitchell Rabin, holistic psychotherapist, host of *A Better World*

Overcoming
TOXIC
EMOTIONS

A PRACTICAL GUIDE
TO BUILDING BETTER RELATIONSHIPS
WITH YOURSELF AND OTHERS

LEAH GUY
INTUITIVE SPIRITUAL HEALER

Skyhorse Publishing

This book is not meant to diagnose, treat, or cure any physical or mental health issues and will not be responsible for such. Please seek medical or professional help if needed or if you are experiencing, or have experienced, abuse of any nature.

Skyhorse Publishing books may be purchased in bulk at special discounts for sales promotion, corporate gifts, fund-raising, or educational purposes. Special editions can also be created to specifications. For details, contact the Special Sales Department, Skyhorse Publishing, 307 West 36th Street, 11th Floor, New York, NY 10018 or info@skyhorsepublishing.com.

Skyhorse® and Skyhorse Publishing® are registered trademarks of Skyhorse Publishing, Inc.®, a Delaware corporation.

Visit our website at www.skyhorsepublishing.com.

10 9 8 7 6 5 4 3 2

Library of Congress Cataloging-in-Publication Data is available on file.

Cover design by Daniel Brount
Cover illustration by Shutterstock

Print ISBN: 978-1-5107-6320-3
Ebook ISBN: 978-1-5107-6321-0

Printed in the United States of America

For all of my clients, students, workshop attendees, and readers—you are brave ones on a self-healing journey and this book is for you. I have learned so much in your presence. In particular, how to listen, how to be a better guide, and how to show up with courage to face deep fears. And mostly, how even though we have different stories, we share a universal language of understanding, hope, and perseverance to reach our highest truth.

Thank you.

Contents

Contents

Introduction
The Hope in Healing

"IT'S not you, it's me."

These words have become a famous exit strategy; words commonly used during a breakup. If you receive these words from your partner, it feels like a dead-end road. There's simply not much you can say or do when the other person takes full responsibility and leaves. It is possible, however, to use these words in your favor with another partner that, unfortunately, many of us have known: Blame.

Break up with blame with the same famous exit strategy. "Blame, this isn't working out. Thanks for your time and what you've taught me. It's going to be hard to leave, but this relationship with you is toxic and isn't working for me any longer. It's nothing you did wrong. It's not you, it's me.

The radical nature of this book is about taking responsibility for why we feel bad, or at least why we aren't having the kind of life experience and relationships that we want. It's about understanding why we push people away, self-sabotage, make excuses, and distract ourselves with busyness.

For the purposes of this book, for recovery, and for changing your life, use the words "It's not you, it's me" as your motto. This isn't a suggestion. To pave the road for personal growth, it's imperative that you take the reins to create the life you desire, and acknowledge that you are the only one who can make your life better. Yes, there are tools to help you (such as this book), but ultimately you hold the key to your own transformation. Many people spend years in therapy attempting to make sense of who did what, why, and when. While therapy can be helpful, spending more time and energy understanding yourself and less time fixating on the other will give you momentum toward self-healing.

"It's not you, it's me" can liberate you to not only accept your feelings without blaming, shaming, accusing, excusing, or projecting, but to actually welcome them with integrity and curiosity. When you dive into your life experience, and see it from this new perspective, everything changes. The story becomes real. And reality shines brighter.

Freedom is both an exhilarating and a terrifying word. We say we want to be free of stress and the same old negative feelings, yet we find ourselves chained inside an inner prison with walls that have entrapped us for too long. Unhappy relationships. Unfulfilling jobs. Debt. Friendships that don't nurture us. Uninspired living situations. We get stuck in the routines of entrapment and blame everything and everyone for keeping us there.

Until we realize we are keeping ourselves in bad situations, nothing will change. Until we realize we are in charge of our lives, nothing will change. Until we realize we can't rewrite the stories of the past, nothing will change.

By stepping into the authority role in your life, you can be free from the chains that bind you. You may visit the internal prison from time to time, but you will not be trapped, defined, or limited by other people's behavior or beliefs, or stuck in the memory of pain any longer.

Are you ready to break up with blame? Are you ready to experience a taste of freedom and happiness in your life?

I hope so. You deserve it.

The Phoenix Rising

The Phoenix Rising analogy was introduced in my first book, *The Fearless Path*, and I often use it in my lectures. It is this energy that I resonate with on my own healing journey, and an analogy that is powerful to embody. I want to remind you of the power of the phoenix that you have within you, and to hold it close to your heart.

The majestic phoenix is a beautiful symbol in mythology that displays pure strength and courage from having fallen into the depths of catastrophe and rising up from the ashes. When the phoenix felt the end was encroaching, it built a nest, lit it on fire, and was then consumed by the flames. From the ashes, the bird arose, powerful and renewed. It's the classic story of rebirth, renewal, and resurrection. We all have the capacity to rise again—to renew our energy and pull ourselves up from the ashes of loss, despair, pain, trauma, and fear—no matter what depths of pain or self-loathing may be present. I believe that because I've been there.

The fires that engulfed my life included experiencing a sexual assault in my early twenties. I had other traumas less definable, and each forced me to essentially leave my body or dissociate in order to deal with the fear. As the flames of despair took over, I became paralyzed, numb to emotion. For a period of time, I was a different person, unrecognizable to myself or to my family and friends. I became depressed, angry, ashamed, and fearful. I didn't want to live. Trauma disrupted my whole life.

In the "fire," my life began spiraling into destruction with alcohol, cigarettes, avoidance, antidepressants, food obsession, and sexual encounters. I cried myself to sleep most nights, or was high on something. My body shame returned from previous unprocessed emotions that cocreated an eating disorder. I over-obsessed about food, and doing anything I could to be seen, while also trying to remain invisible. I was living in constant conflict within myself and I hated my life. I hated the people who violated me so deeply. I hated most things. This was one of the lowest of lows I had ever experienced and I was desperate to get up.

Thankfully, I did get up. I'm not going to lie and say it was a spontaneous resurrection. It was an ongoing process fueled by connection, commitment, and the steps you're going to work through in this book. If I can get through it, I believe you can too. Your story may be different than mine, and whatever your story or history, it is validated here. Too often we don't validate the feelings of the experiences that we had, and we must start there. We all need support, and my intention is to be one of the supports in your life. Lean on these words, do the steps, and believe that change is possible. Because change *is* possible!

The biggest contributions you can make to your journey of renewal and reconstruction are:

1. Honesty
2. Commitment
3. Connection

If you aren't completely honest with your feelings, behaviors, needs, and past history, it will be impossible to make true transformation in your life. We get really good at creating semi-truths, saying what others expect, suffocating or diminishing our needs, and making excuses for the people or situations that hurt us. It's time to step into raw vulnerability with yourself and become a truth-teller. This alone is a powerful step.

It's not uncommon to commit to many other things and people except ourselves. Let's change that starting now. Your self-loyalty will be key in creating new boundaries, trusting yourself, and building confidence to rise up strong. It's not just the act of commitment, it's the energy and intention of commitment that sends a subconscious message to self that says, *I am worthy!*

If there is one thing we all need in life, it is connection. From birth and throughout all phases of our lives, we thrive on support from people, nature, sound, touch, and spiritual connection. So before you read any further, I want you to think about how to stay connected to these resources and make them a part of your daily experience. No one thrives in a desert without water. (Except cacti. You are not a cactus.)

Let's focus on reconstructing the pieces of your life that feel stuck, broken, or negative. You aren't broken. You, like others, have had difficult or traumatic experiences, heartbreak, or hurt that left you feeling disempowered, worthless, afraid, and small. The good news is you can shift those patterns that up to now have been difficult to change. It takes mental fortitude to understand the lasting impact that negative experiences have had on your well-being. Before you know it, you will dismantle the system of self-sabotage and be on a path of reconstructing an empowering, healthy, and happy life.

How do you get there?

If you want to heal now, this book is for you. Many self-help books leave the reader with great understanding but no practical plan for how to make the changes needed to move forward. Here, I provide you with a simple, effective, no-nonsense approach to healing using my AAA Method: Acknowledge. Accept. Act.

You may think, *Oh, yeah, I know those words,* and dismiss the transformational process ahead. Don't jump to conclusions. Please give these words a chance. Move through the work with me and apply the AAA Method. You will gain a new perspective of those words, and your relationship to self will change.

The AAA Method is a facilitator of healing that creates a new landscape where you can flourish and manifest. It will excavate stagnant, blocked energy that has been choking off your life force. The AAA Method actually becomes fun to apply, and it is amazing to witness the shift from "toxic vibes" to #goodvibes.

There is power in rewriting our imprints, learning new behavioral patterns, and healing the parts of us that hurt. If you apply my simple three-step method in your personal healing work, you can be successful in shifting negative emotions, eliminating false beliefs, alleviating trauma responses, and gaining self-confidence.

The AAA Method will give you a strategy to implement, while also guiding you to discover your emotional imprints and vibrational frequencies that have kept you addicted to negative patterns and behaviors. You will learn how to reframe your stories, raise your vibration, and create a new energetic matrix that will lead you to a different life experience.

There is some heavy lifting in this book, but I will make it as straightforward as possible so you can have a system of success. The AAA Method can help you discover or reclaim healthy and positive relationships if you experience any of the following emotions or behaviors in your life:

- Emotionally stuck, trapped, lost, or blocked
- Repeating negative relationships or attracting negative people
- Unable to make decisions or move forward in positive/ productive ways
- Negative self-talk or beliefs about body image
- Feeling invalidated, unseen, or unheard
- Unable to say no or to create healthy boundaries
- Feeling responsible for other people's happiness or wellness
- Deep anger or resentment, inability to forgive
- A need to control others
- Lack of confidence and fear of rejection
- Unsafe, fearful, or anxious
- Unsure of your purpose or why you are here

Within this book, you will identify the toxic emotions that have controlled you, the stories from which they originated, and how you've dealt with negative experiences in your life. These factors have significant impact on your mental, emotional, and energetic health. You will learn how to use principles of vibration and mindfulness to overcome toxic patterns.

Moving forward on the path to recovery requires attention to the ways your inner child has been affected and how that continues to affect you in adulthood. By utilizing the AAA Method, you will then learn to accept and reidentify your authentic self, re-parent your inner child, and move toward healing.

About Toxic Emotions

We all want to belong, feel purposeful, and be loved. Seems easy enough, but for most people it's a constant (and often secret) struggle. Low self-worth bred by negative belief patterns and unhealthy emotions get in the way. Resentments, fear, anger, and deep traumatic experiences make us recoil, lash out, or attempt to sidestep an emotion that threatens our well-being. We've grown so used to our pain that we begin a pattern of resistance, which can easily turn into self-sabotage or sabotaging relationships.

Toxic emotions infect every area of our lives: relationships, careers, mental health, physical health, family systems, and quality of life. It's easy to point the finger and give name(s) or history as the reason for our misery. However, these are defense mechanisms we use to avoid a deeper sense of worthlessness.

Negative and toxic emotions are learned behavior either from our family of origin, environment, or how we were treated. We may have collected ancestral stories and trauma experiences passed down from generation to generation. There is a great difference between your true nature and learned behavior, and my goal is to help you realign with your higher self, your true nature, and heal the pain that has accumulated throughout your life.

Have you ever asked yourself any of these questions?

"Why do I feel insecure?"
"Why am I not as strong as everyone thinks I am?"
"Why do I feel like a child who hasn't fully matured?"
"Why am I afraid of rejection?"
"Why do I keep hurting myself?"
"I'm a smart person, so why can't I break this cycle?"

"Why am I afraid that no one will love me if I'm not doing something for them?"
"Why don't I like myself?"
"Why do I feel small and invisible?"

Asking why doesn't provide the answer, nor does understanding why offer a full resolution, but it's a place to start so we can dig a bit deeper and understand our emotional patterns or imprints.

Although you may have the urge to believe negative truths, you aren't at fault for your less-than-perfect behaviors or tendencies. You are just responding to pain and suffering in unhealthy ways. The fact that you're reading this book is a testament to the love you have for yourself and others. And that love is making you brave, strong, able, and willing to experience life in a new way. Love says you are worthy, and that is where to focus. If you start feeding the pattern of believing negative truths, just take a pause and say to yourself, *Wait, I'm working on my life. I'm brave, strong, able, and willing to do this. My attempt is proof that love is in me. I am worthy.*

Your fear response is normal. Backing away, repressing, hiding, blaming, anger, denial—these are all normal responses to pain, because you are trying to protect yourself from more pain. But because of these fear responses you may have developed unhealthy patterns that are destructive to your best life. While sometimes we feel we need to isolate, control, defend, or protect these behaviors, in reality, these behaviors only serve to keep us stuck. If you want more from your life and are craving the sweet freedom of ease, joy, peace, and love, reading this book will improve your awareness of your own fear-based behaviors and give you steps to heal.

The stories we believe about ourselves dominate how we operate. If those stories are filled with shame, guilt, or negative beliefs, we get stuck in those emotions. We continue those negative patterns into adulthood with self-sabotage. We may act out in attempts to be seen, heard, and validated, or we act in ways that continue the cycle of pain that has become so comfortable. In this book we will separate our stories from our truths, and reframe our perspectives.

We become addicted to the pain that binds us. As uncomfortable as it is, or as much pain as you've experienced in abuse, neglect, or emotional suffocation, negative feelings resonate a particular vibration within your cells, memory, and tissues. These are your imprints. Up till now, at least. Your experience of feeling a certain way and your sense of worth and fear are tied to this pattern, and although you know it doesn't feel "good" or "right," it has become comfortable. Don't mistake this kind of comfort with warm-cozy-fuzzy comfort. There's nothing cozy about pain. But comfort comes from a pattern of familiarity, and over time we accept pain as normal and reliable. We feed off it.

Operating from your imprint, you continue attracting unhealthy relationships and experiences—or at least recreating scenarios that are oh-so-familiar—that allow you to continue feeling the way you've been conditioned to feel. It's the law of attraction. Round and round you go with the toxic game of self-destruction.

In this book you will dive deeper into your inner world to shake loose the grips of negative emotions that are weighing you down. As you begin taking responsibility for your happiness, you step into the authority role to become a changemaker in your own life. This is exhilarating work. Although tapping into your authenticity often forces you to face fear, and asks you to transform resentment, you can then transcend the muck and mire of your wounds into wings of relief and joy.

This work provides the knowledge and tools to change your emotional and energetic imprints from early childhood and create a new vibration that will manifest a different life. It is possible to reignite your passion and engage in safe, intimate relationships with yourself and others. When you use the AAA Method, you have the tools needed to succeed.

The self-care exercises in this book are focused on creating healthy boundaries, opening your heart to get unstuck in relationship patterns, and adopting a connection to your true nature. This includes relationship patterns with your higher self so you can change the energy and trajectory of how you relate to others. You may want to set aside a separate journal or at least have something handy to jot down notes and do the exercises as you read.

A personal note: To follow the same principles I ask of you, I use my stories, and those of friends or clients with permission, as a way to be honest about where I've been and where I am now and to stay present and committed on my path. I am not a general with no battle scars. I'm on the field, right here with you. And in that, we stay connected.

So, I thank you in advance for not only accepting who I am, but also having the wisdom to apply these stories to your own life. As a healing practitioner, I hear many stories, and I learn from each one. It's community that provides empathy for the struggles of our humanity. We are all in this together, and we learn and help each other.

You can count on me to be on your team. You are a fierce and strong warrior. Claim that for yourself now and you'll be on your way to creating healthier, happier relationships with yourself and others.

I'm so glad you are here!

Your friend,

Leah

Chapter 1
Identify Toxic Emotions That Have Controlled Your Life

LIFE can be so amazing, awe-inspiring, and beautiful. We have much to be grateful for: an Earth that provides food and natural resources, unlimited potential for growth, and most everything that a person needs to function and thrive. But at the same time, we've each been given very different and often difficult experiences. It's like the gift of life comes with its own bag of stinky manure. Everyone's experience is unique, but none without its own cruelty. And no one is immune to it. We try to negotiate the weight of our circumstances as we navigate through life, occasionally getting a fresh whiff of the stench along the way.

Although it's unfortunate what many of us must deal with in life, there can be value in hardship. It's through wrestling with issues of our heart and mind that we grow, become more empathic, compassionate, and come to realize what worth really means—the worth of a moment, a sunset, or even love. And, hopefully, we come to acknowledge our own worth and purpose in the world.

The best way to reduce the negative impact of our experience is to till that bag of dung like a good composter would for his garden. As we process painful experiences, and work new experiences in, we fertilize and nurture our lives, helping to resolve the tightly bound toxic soil, allowing new roots to spread and oxygen to enliven our cells. Emotional composting makes our internal environment less likely to erode, and prevents the spread of disease. Once you acknowledge and accept this process, you will become empowered to rise up from the ashes and soar. The goal of this book is to help you learn how to respond differently to the life you've been given.

Now, getting to those toxic emotions. A recent meme on Instagram said, "The *only* toxic relationship I ever had was the one I had with myself . . . everyone else was just a reflection of that." What truth. What power! There's nothing more prickly, yucky, or uncomfortable than long-held toxic emotions. It's like unhealthy balls of trapped energy circulating through your body, wreaking havoc on your entire system. The stress of negative emotions can weaken the heart, immune, digestive, and respiratory systems, as well as your mental health. You may feel like you can't clear your mind, as negative thought patterns are hard to stop. Sometimes toxic emotions feel dirty, like you are unclean. You may feel unattractive and don't want others to see you fully or get too close. These common physical sensations reflect unhealthy emotions that are not meant to be stored in the body for long.

Emotions can become so difficult to manage that we wrestle with them inside for years, developing our own toxic coping mechanisms such as self-abandonment, betrayal, or abuse. We create more shameful experiences, overcontrol our lives, or bury our emotions in order to tolerate ourselves and maintain a familiar identity, even if that identity is not healthy or positive.

Toxic emotions confine us in a silent prison. Breaking up with blame is the key to freedom. To start, let's be honest with ourselves and identify the emotions that control us. Most toxic emotions are developed from false beliefs attached to core wounds that have manifested in depth. Some of these beliefs may be that we are not good enough (worthy of being loved), that we don't belong (we don't matter or feel safe in the world), or that we are responsible for other people's feelings (guilty for being imperfect, not allowed to make mistakes).

Unprocessed, unhealthy emotions that are left ignored will become toxic to your system. It's not the spouse, the money, the parents, the boss, the amount of (or lack of) time, or the kids. It's us. I'll stop repeating this soon, but sometimes our psyches need repetitive reassurances to grasp a new concept. The emotional pains that we've collected and not processed keep us in unhealthy, unhappy loops. It's your job to identify the toxic emotions so you can begin to clear them.

The most difficult step toward healing is taking responsibility for how you feel. It's hard, but it's also empowering. You can start right now by saying "This is mine now. And I will make changes in my life for the betterment of me." When you release the need to project and blame, you step into the fast lane of growth.

This work isn't about victimizing yourself or becoming a martyr. Victims and martyrs cannot survive in the space of self-healing because being a victim or a martyr drains your power and creates bypasses around personal growth. Don't allow anyone to walk all over you. That drains your power. Don't excuse other people's behavior, even if you think they did the best they could. That also drains your power. Transformation that lasts comes from integrity, and it results in the highest vibration of health.

The healing process begins with deep, sometimes uncomfortable reflection. We shift into healing the same way we shifted into self-destruction, by accepting the thoughts and feelings we have about ourselves. Self-destructive thoughts and feelings were learned by experiencing shame, being ignored, neglected, or abused. Self-healing thoughts and feelings are learned by feeling worthy, validated, seen, and loved. The only difference is that we are no longer reliant on others to feed us what we need.

First, remember not to judge yourself for how you feel. The goal is to feel better, but let's not make our negative feelings our foes. They are necessary to teach and guide us, but they shouldn't dominate everything else. Negative emotions are natural but unprocessed negative emotions become toxic.

Next, be clear about the actual negative emotions you experience. You may feel bad or not good enough, but you need to identify the driving force behind those emotions so you can heal the actual cause. You may say you "feel" ugly, fat, or broken. Though you may experience a feeling of brokenness, you are not broken. "Broken" isn't an emotion, just like "fat" isn't an emotion. Ugly, fat, and broken are not feelings, but ways to bypass the real emotion that is harder to access such as shame or anguish.

Think of yourself as an investigator of your authentic experience so you can give close attention to that which needs healing and move forward in a healthy and happy fashion. You must first identify what emotions are, and how you cover them up with words that continue the cycle of blame, denial, and distraction. You're going to get to know yourself in a brand-new way, and that's the exciting part of healing.

Carroll Izard at the University of Delaware developed a list of valid emotions as measured in his Differential Emotions Scale (DES-IV). This list is widely referenced in the medical and educational communities and I've found it to be useful in my own practice.

List of Valid Emotions

Joy	Anguish
Interest	Contempt
Anger	Guilt
Fear	Shyness
Disgust	Sadness
Shame	Self-hostility

Izard's list may be surprisingly short, but it's important to note that other emotions are closely related to or fall under the same emotions above. We will also address surface feelings that create unpleasant experiences and lead to toxicity. Feelings are the conscious experience of emotional reactions. For the sake of clarity, I will refer to both emotions and feelings interchangeably so as to address all aspects of potential issues.

Notice that love is not on the list. Love is considered a choice, not an emotion or feeling. American psychiatrist and bestselling author of *The Road Less Traveled* M. Scott Peck believes that love is a behavior, too. If you choose love, it's normal to have a range of emotions and feelings due to the experience of love. It's common to register emotions and feelings as physical experiences (which means that emotional experiences can lead to physical pain and disease).

Remember me asking you to commit to that first level of honesty? Here we are. There's no longer reason to color past events or feelings. When we lie, we hurt ourselves first. When we speak truth, we heal ourselves first. There's no rationale, excuse, or explanation needed. This journey of exploration is to reveal the heart of what pains you, and to acknowledge the truth of that experience for yourself.

When you acknowledge what you truly feel, you may experience that familiar urge to hold others responsible. If you ever get the urge to blame others for *why* you feel the way you feel, come back to that famous breakup line and think, *Blame, it's not you, it's me.* We all want to feel justified in our feelings and existence, but when we blame or deny, we are blocked from true healing. Remember, blaming gives most of your power to the other person.

We want to learn to reclaim our power. This doesn't mean you won't acknowledge where things may have started to go wrong. It doesn't mean you take responsibility for everything bad that has happened to you, or look away from the people who may have hurt you. It simply means that both now, and in the future, you learn to stay present with reality as you know it and own the way you feel. Only you can own your behaviors, thoughts, emotions, and choices. It's impossible to change something you don't own.

It's scary to give up the reason for your feeling and just feel. It's scary to relinquish the offender of responsibility and own your reality. What this really does is release you from the power that any other person has over you. Let the person who hurt you deal with the repercussions of their actions. This mind shift helps you take control of your choices and allows the other person to control theirs. Keep your focus on taking care of you, not fixing or getting even with them. If your energy isn't given to them any longer, you have more energy to heal the pain that binds you.

Every interaction and relationship serves a purpose. Everything, for better or worse, either helps you learn and grow, or justifies your positive or negative beliefs about yourself. Keep the following questions in mind, as they will be used again on page 13:

1. If you struggle with a difficult relationship or toxic person in your life, what do you bring to this relationship? What attitudes, beliefs, wounds, and expectations do you carry?
2. How is this relationship or person serving you? What is the reason you are allowing that person to stay in your life?

You may want to jot down some initial thoughts in your journal before you read further.

Being curious about yourself and situations allows you to ask the question "why" without bringing on the knee-jerk reactions of blame, defensiveness, distancing, or anxiety. Why do you stay in situations, jobs, and relationships that don't serve your health or highest good? Are you validating limited beliefs of worthlessness or pain? Is the other person or situation reflecting a positive image of you and encouraging your potential, or are they confirming fears that you aren't worthy to be loved, successful, and happy? You may begin to see patterns of self-sabotage that you didn't realize were at play.

You've likely heard people say, "They made me feel _____" or "She makes me so mad I can't see straight." If someone "makes you feel" angry, there is stored anger energy within you that hasn't been addressed. If someone "makes you feel" small or weak, there is an emotional imprint of weakness that is being triggered by the other person.

The truth is, people can't "make you feel" anything. They can say and do things to trigger you, push your buttons, attempt to aggravate or affect you, but you are responsible for how you feel. From here forward, I will put the phrase "make(s) you feel/made me feel" in quotes to remind us that this is an old pattern of thinking, not a truth.

If someone has ever apologized to you saying, "I'm sorry, I didn't mean to hurt your feelings," imagine the power you'd feel if you replied, "You didn't!" When we have strong tools in place, we can separate the actual words and intentions of the other, look at our patterns, and recover without blame.

Let's take a look at rejection. If rejection feels like a pain you cannot bear, a circumstance you'll do anything to avoid, it's likely you have a history of feeling left out and unloved, or at least wondered *Why doesn't someone pick me for their team?* in the past. In other words, if rejection is a toxic feeling that sits inside of you due to unprocessed pain of shame, then any form of rejection feels intolerable and terrifying because there's history there.

There's a deep fear, in this instance, that rejection will confirm to you that you are rejectable and that you aren't worthy of someone's time, love, and commitment. To be rejected again would confirm that you are not worthy or lovable. When core wounds come from people we love and trust the most, it can start a firestorm of emotions that cut deeply. It's a feeling that everyone tries to avoid, and why we do a song and dance with our emotional prisoners in attempt to control the shame we experience. You may subconsciously think, *Don't let anyone see what I know: I am not good enough for you to stay.*

Why would we want to keep away from wholeness and joy? We don't. But emotional addiction is real, and addiction to pain is hard to break without guidance. The AAA Method will help.

AAA Method

A surefire system to begin processing and shifting negative emotions is my AAA Method. It's like an insurance policy to assure you are moving toward self-love and healing, instead of harboring negative experiences and staying in old patterns.

The AAA Method includes three steps:

1. Acknowledgment
2. Acceptance
3. Action

Throughout this book you will be applying these steps. When resistance, hesitation, anger, defensiveness, or self-sabotage kicks in, pause and use the Method. Consistency will help you not only gain self-confidence, but feel more in control as you begin the process of rewriting your emotional imprints and raising your vibration. The process works like this:

Acknowledgment

The first step in making a change is to acknowledge what is true. Acknowledgment is powerful. If you received the acknowledgments you desired for all the jobs and efforts you accomplished throughout your life, they would have made a positive and lasting impact. Acknowledgment creates firmness and clarity in your reality whereas ignoring a situation keeps you in denial.

If you can find the courage to own and acknowledge the truth about how you feel, such as "I am full of resentment," or "I feel . . ." then you are on your way to healing. What isn't productive is "I am full of resentment *because* . . . " Now, you're blaming and denying.

Acknowledgment sounds simple, like the other steps in the AAA Method. However, being truthful and able to see reality without judgment, blaming, or excuses can be challenging because these negative responses are reflexes we've learned to defend ourselves. Unlearning these negative responses may take time.

Acceptance

Acceptance is applying acknowledgment, understanding, and compassion to a feeling, and giving it room to just be. In accepting the actual feeling or behavior we experience in the present moment of reality, all of our energy becomes available to move forward, even if that means just sitting with the truth. Acceptance makes space for reality, offers grace for the limits of our humanity, aligns the mind and emotions, and encourages self-love.

Don't move too fast through acceptance. It must be genuine and felt throughout the body in order to have the power we need to transform. The mind and heart must be in agreement with acceptance, and once the acceptance is complete, there is no going back to denial (excuses, old stories, past experiences).

Action

Action is about forward motion toward a new thought, emotion, or energy. Action doesn't have to include physical movement, although sometimes it might. It may be an internal and personal action (forming new beliefs, taking deep breaths, practicing healthy behavior), or at times action may be following through on major life decisions. I find that the most sustainable and practical types of action for the purpose of self-growth are what I call micro-steps. Small, steady movements toward a new outcome. As long as you are committed to the process, and get creative along the way, you will be successful. I offer examples of the AAA Method in action throughout this book, but it may be helpful to make written reminders for yourself that you are dedicated to healing.

Before we go much further, I'd like to identify some words or terms that will be used frequently in this book so we can have a similar understanding.

Core Wounds

Our beliefs about our worth, our value, and who we are as individuals are based on the interactions and behaviors of how others treated us as very small children. Core wounds are devastating negative beliefs brought on by childhood experiences that have created emotional or mental pain in adulthood. Core wounds disrupt optimal health and feelings of safety, unconditional love, or connection.

False (or Limited) Beliefs

False or limited beliefs are things we may believe that are not true. These can originate from adopting beliefs from our parents or family members without discerning their truth. They also come from limiting our understanding of self or the world due to our own insecurities or the lack of encouragement to be curious, explore, and attain autonomy. False beliefs are untruths, meaning they may be someone else's opinions, but not factual information. If someone else's opinions are not healthy or positive, these beliefs affect our understanding about self and worth.

Emotional Imprints

Emotional imprints are the emotions and thoughts that house our belief system. Imprints are formed in our developmental years from the information we gathered through life experience, creating lasting effects on how we operate and view the world today.

Vibrational Frequencies

Everything is energy. We vibrate at various frequencies depending on our state of health, environment, and mental and emotional beliefs. Every emotion and thought resonates with a certain frequency. Lower vibrational frequencies generally feel dense, heavy, or negative, in body, mind, and heart. Higher vibrational frequencies feel lighter, brighter, and more aligned with positive feelings in body, mind, and heart.

Inner Child

Your inner child is a part of you that lives within, carried forward by memory of the innocent childlike state. Your developmental maturity may have been stunted at a certain age depending on trauma, unmet emotional needs, or other difficult experiences that you were not able to mentally or emotionally process. Your inner child may become emotionally activated during times of stress or fear in the adult self.

Higher Self

Your higher self is the part of you most aligned with your divine nature that recognizes your deserving attributes, beauty, and power. It is the wisdom that is guided by your soul to embody your true nature.

Emotional Trauma

Emotional trauma is damage done to your psyche (and emotional or physical bodies) after experiencing a devastatingly stressful or frightening life event. Although many people associate trauma with major life occurrences such as abuse or shock, trauma in this book also refers to the deeply impactful feelings a situation or event causes in which a child or adult is not able to process the pain, fear, threat, or betrayal.

Giving Your Power Away

Ownership is power. The ownership of your truth is your power. And without power on your side, you'll be mired in mud for years, weighed down by the stories of your past. It will always be "Sally's" fault. Or Mom's fault. Or your hubby's fault. The "It's not you, it's me" mentality will free you from blaming any person, place, or thing to make yourself feel better.

If you are focused on the outside world, not only do you become drained of energy and lose your power, but your fortress of toxic emotions also grows higher. This system of toxicity may seem natural or reasonable given past circumstances, but now that you are free to make your own life choices, you see that unhealthy reactions and self-sabotage are just defense mechanisms to keep you away from wholeness and joy.

If you allow it, others can drain your energy. Especially if you have a history of feeling used, manipulated, or abused, it's easy to give so much power to another person. When we blame the other person who has "taken our power," we are really mad at ourselves for not having enough control over our choices. Defensiveness is the weaker position; it's not the simplest, but it is the weakest.

Let's take your power back. In giving our power away we think we're losing and the other person is gaining, but neither is true. It's one thing to give energy to people who ask for our time or help like when a friend calls or when we volunteer for an organization. It's nice when friends or loved ones reach out. But most people give their energy to people when it isn't asked for or wanted, and then accuse them of not caring, or hurting us if they don't want our help, opinions, or caretaking.

No one should give their energy to people who haven't asked for it. It only serves your need to wait on the acceptance and approval of others. You wait to know that they may need you, which validates your existence because you haven't learned to give it to yourself. Yet.

Notice the number of thoughts you have about other people or situations that are out of your control. It is likely staggering. Fixating on what someone else may be doing solves nothing. Worry gets you nowhere. Waiting for someone to call doesn't make them call. It only gives you the comfort of addiction—waiting on the acceptance and approval of others. This continued cycle of addiction to pain allows you to bypass your own emotions and issues.

If you wonder why you feel so drained, empty, invisible, used, or betrayed, it is because you are draining your vital energy on others in an attempt to avoid your discomfort and unhealed core wounds. You have unhealthy attachments to a perceived sense of love and belonging, which stop you from feeding healthy energy to self and balanced relationships. You aren't exhausted from doing too much, you're exhausted from giving your energy to the wrong thing.

I would estimate that my clients talk about someone else in their life for about 75 percent of the time during our initial sessions. They tell me about their spouse and what he/she did or said and then they look at me to validate their belief about the other. I get it, because what people say and do can have a great impact, so much so that I've written a book about the impact of others on us. But in order to make change in your life and relationships, you have to keep steering the focus back to you. I must remind my clients that the sessions are about them, not the other person. We can only grow so much by understanding the behaviors or history of another. It can help rationalize situations, but it can't help process our own emotional wounds. Focusing too much on others can be the greatest distraction from our own growth.

Let's get back to those earlier questions on page 6 about what you bring to a difficult or toxic relationship, and how that toxic relationship serves you. By serving, I don't necessarily mean that the relationship is serving your highest good and it feels beneficial. All too often, toxic relationships facilitate our negative feelings and feed our addiction to a lower vibration. And somehow this becomes strangely comfortable.

If you're feeling reactive and triggered at the thought of releasing the hook from another person (or breaking up with blame) to attend to your own happiness, this is a good sign that you're in the right place.

You can put this book down and do things the way you've been doing them. You can keep making rationalizations for all the reasons you feel slighted, lonely, angry, rejected, or resentful. You can blame or deny, and look at the world and see all of the ways it has hurt you and all of the potential it has to take you down.

Or you can keep reading and awaken to a different aspect of yourself. The part of you who wants to be unchained, whole, and happy.

Don't get me wrong, self-healing isn't all about self-blaming. It's not *all* about you. It never is. There is always you and the other, and the impact of the other is great. The way you've been treated has mattered, for good or bad. And it's important to acknowledge it honestly and squarely. There's a very good reason for why you feel the way you feel.

What we want to change is what is happening inside of you, now.

Making change must be fueled by self-love and preservation or it won't last. Change fueled by trying to prove someone wrong or to get revenge isn't healthy motivation. It's like dieting for the temporary beach vacation instead of committing to a permanent healthy lifestyle.

Although this work is about your personal transformation, I can assure you of one thing: as you make positive changes in your life, it will affect your relationships with everyone around you. So, as a by-product, this work will make an impact on others, or at least how you experience them. That's a good thing.

Making a commitment to change is scary. It's the unknown that we're afraid of and the departure from the norm. This may bring up anxiety, resentments, anger, and grief. To transform, we have to navigate new and rocky terrain until we become more familiar with a new perspective and belief system.

Trauma is real. I believe many of us have far more residual trauma from relationships and family issues than we recognize. What's hard for many people is getting started because of the fears that emerge. The deeper the trauma, or the longer you've functioned from a place of fear, the more intense this work will be. Let's take it one step at a time, and keep the focus on you versus the event or the other person.

There's nothing wrong with difficult feelings. Anger, jealousy, dislike, fear, disappointment, shame, and guilt all have their place in teaching us something about ourselves, or a relationship, or life. Emotions are meant to be fluid, moving in and out of our senses as they are experienced. You can always trust that emotions will circle back, as they should, because you need access to the full range of emotions to experience life. It's holding on to a negative emotion that gets you into trouble.

Allowing difficult feelings to process through our emotional bodies will bring us to a healthier place. It feels risky, I know. But once you move through the fear of feeling and gain self-confidence, you can then experience a fuller range of emotions such as joy, peace, self-trust, and compassion.

Our toxic emotions reinforce the belief that we are not worthy enough to be happy. Happiness doesn't match our current vibrational level. We do not trust ourselves, or others, to care for us and not harm us because we don't believe we are valuable. This internal dialogue is critical, hateful, and self-sabotaging. We live in conflict because we can't foster a healthy ego and a sense of worth against the shame, fear, and pain we feel. For some of us, this can blossom into self-loathing, isolation, or codependency. At the extreme, it can become full-blown personality disorders.

Identifying Toxic Emotions

Toxic emotions are the result of unprocessed feelings that have been repressed or ignored for too long. Without overanalyzing, which words stand out to you? Write them down. It can be one or several, but choose without judgment. Choose with your body. Which words cause immediate visceral sensations? Which cause emotional reactions? Which ones make you sad or give you a sinking feeling?

Ashamed	Worthless	Regret
Irritated	Disappointment	Dejected
Resentful	Insecure	Frustration
Heartbroken	Envy	Abnormal
Guilt	Overwhelmed	Depression
Insensitive	Self-absorption	Deprived
Bitterness	Lonely	Anger
Manipulated	Empty	Threatened
Hatred	Incapable	Apathy
Powerless	Denial	Dissatisfaction
Self-loathing	Hostile	Pain
Tormented	Anxiety	Self-criticism
Fear	Helpless	Blaming others

Isolation	Negativity	Bitterness
Chronic complaining	Jealousy	Vengeful
Feeling like a victim	Sadness	Aggressive
Distrust	Despair	

Of those you picked, separate three or four that are most familiar, and have traveled with you throughout many of your relationships and life experiences. We will work with these as part of your core wound(s).

If you had a hard time picking your top three from the list, past experiences can help lead you directly to the toxic emotions that are affecting your life. Think of your most toxic relationship and what you might have said in the past if you were to explain how that person "made you feel." Now, take that feeling and match it to the toxic emotions that come up for you.

Sit with these words and feelings for a few moments, stare at them on the page, and then speak and give them your full attention and acknowledgment. Can you then move into a place of accepting them? Use your inner voice, and with your heart say "I see you, and I accept you" to these toxic emotions. It may be uncomfortable, but you won't make progress until you can truly accept what is.

Remember, all negative emotions are natural to the degree that they relate to a particular event or circumstance, but if held internally for too long they will become toxic. Are you holding on to any of these out of fear of more suffering? Are you being honest with yourself right now, or do you feel defensive? Are you itching to explain and blame?

It's natural if part of your brain wants to categorize to make sense of things. Let it. Then come back to yourself, your feelings, and your behaviors and repeat the breakup mantra: "Blame, it's not working out anymore. It's not you, it's me. Thanks for all you've taught me, but I'm going to move along now and take care of myself."

You aren't here to fix anyone else. In fact, you can't. That's their job. Just like they can't "make you feel." You can only address your own experiences and work to have better and more consistent feelings of strength, peace, and love.

Take control of you.

Let's Talk About Shame and Guilt

Shame and guilt are two toxic emotions that many of us carry. They are the most common core wounds. And they are like siblings from a dysfunctional family, one often feeding the other in a vicious cycle.

- I'm not worthy/good/good enough/enough. (Shame)
- I don't belong/I'm different/People don't accept me/I'm not like them. (Shame)
- If I were different, I would be loved/understood/validated. (Guilt)
- I am too much/too sensitive/too ignorant/too slow/too fast. (Shame *and* guilt)

Many negative emotions are rooted in shame and/or guilt, and these are common self-loathing messages that most people have grappled with at one time or another. As toxicity sets in, these messages become constant.

Without understanding the origin of shame or guilt, we cannot move into a state of health. The trickiest thing about shame and guilt is that our inner child absorbed the energy of these emotions and created false beliefs that we continue to believe as adults, even if we have no clear idea as to why we feel the way we do.

Shame and guilt lead to the abandonment of our dreams, and detachment from our relationships. These emotions decrease our worth and create negative self-talk that hinders healthy decisions and cause us to measure ourselves against others; being not as "good/pretty/skinny/smart/wealthy/funny" as they are, or as we "should" be.

Believing we should live for others can also be rooted in shame or guilt and becomes ingrained in our psyche. This way of living is accepted by our social systems, making it hard to identify healthy behavior. Our career choices, family decisions, creative expression, and even how we dress often stem from societal expectations. Asking ourselves "Who am I?" is not as encouraged as asking "If I do it this way, will I be accepted?"

Now, looking at the words you selected and applying the statements of shame or guilt, from where does your toxic emotion stem?

- I'm not worthy/good/good enough/enough. (Shame)
- I don't belong/I'm different/People don't accept me/I'm not like them. (Shame)
- If I were different I would be loved/understood/validated. (Guilt)
- I am too much/too sensitive/too ignorant/too slow/too fast. (Shame *and* guilt)

You may be tapping into fear with these emotions, and that's okay. Fear can be a signal that things are changing within you and that you are ready to step out of your comfort zone. Applying the AAA Method will help you feel more at ease.

AAA Method
Acknowledge that you fear a core wound of shame or guilt.
Accept the presence of fear associated with shame or guilt by allowing it to be real and felt in your body.

Take **action** to move through the fear with a small step such as doing an activity you are good at to boost your confidence and self-love.

A Deeper Look at Shame and Guilt

If you suffer from low self-worth or lack of determination, it's possible that shame and/or guilt are core wounds for you emotionally, and they could be the source of your pain. Working with these elements is critical to healing.

Shame affects the development of your ego and sense of self. If you did not have healthy interactions in your formative years, where you received validation, encouragement, compassion, and healthy boundaries, it's likely that you do not have the muscle to demonstrate appropriate nurturing for others (and yourself) as an adult. Many with a shame wound lack confidence in self, or ability to express their authentic nature. It becomes a daily battle to accept their worth or operate from a place of high self-esteem.

When we are healthily supported as children, we learn to self-soothe, and offer compassion and forgiveness to the self and others. We are gifted with a mirror of love and acceptance, a positive sense of self, and are able to claim our worth. Unfortunately, too many children do not have this experience.

Most children are sensitive and loving, constantly watching their parents or siblings and reacting to their experiences. When a child is routinely criticized, yelled at, ignored, or in any way abused, the child interprets these actions and develops shame, a belief that something is wrong with them, and their parent's upset is their fault.

As children, many of us felt like we were not heard, validated, or encouraged. Life issues such as competing siblings, a lack of money, addicted parents, divorce, emotional separation, or constant turmoil led to fewer family connections or little to no physical and emotional nurturing.

As you dig into your emotional history and energetic patterns, you may recognize difficult relationships, especially with your parents or childhood friends and mentors. If the person you relied on to care for and love you unconditionally didn't provide a safe way for you to witness yourself and others, or you weren't emotionally nurtured as a child, you undoubtedly feel a void in your adult life. Your breakup with those negative feelings begins here.

While all children can drive their parents to anger or frustration (parenting is not easy), repetitive behavior from the parent is not always attributed to the child's actions. Unpleasant glances that scream "I don't approve," questioning the child's ability, yelling, blaming, talking down to, hitting, emotional neglect, emotional manipulation, expecting too much, criticizing body image—these types of destructive interactions leave a lasting impact on children.

Parents with addictions, verbally or emotionally abusive parents, emotionally unavailable parents, parents who abandoned their child, or narcissistic parents are some of the most difficult experiences for children that leave them feeling angry, ashamed, resentful, and unlovable. Even parents who loved deeply but couldn't be present in their child's life can contribute to that child's confused and unhealthy relationship with self and others. It misinforms that child in his or her developmental years as to what healthy love and care looks and feels like.

Children have great empathy, and they may feel guilty and shamed when they can't help their loved ones. While they care deeply for their parent who is dysfunctional or pained, children are also motivated to fix the problem so that they themselves can be loved in the way they need. This is a survival skill, rather than a selfish or conscious knowing at that age. Children yearn to have a present parent, a happy parent, and a functional and peaceful parent. Striving to win their parent's attention and approval is too great of a burden for a child to bear.

When a parent suffers mentally, emotionally, or physically, children will often try to take on adult responsibility that isn't theirs. They may take on the parenting role with their siblings, become an emotionally surrogate spouse, or a parent's best friend or confidant. This can be true for children of divorced parents as well. Their developing minds and hearts are too young to make sense of the upset, loss, or trauma they witnessed, but their empathetic instinct is to help.

Many adults struggle to hold their parents responsible even after years of their own suffering. They make excuses such as "They did the best they could." "I believe they loved me even though they never hugged me or told me they did." The fear of owning our pains and their origins can feel like a violation to our own blood but it's very important to remember that you are not blaming. You are acknowledging and accepting your past pains so that you can accurately assess toxic patterns in order to move forward. Creating barriers by rationalizing the deficits of others only serves to minimize your own truth, disempowering you from healing.

The Language of Guilt

Many people believe they don't suffer from guilt. My clients often tell me they don't feel guilt when they tap into their negative behaviors. But guilt can manifest in a myriad of ways: as the need to be in control, take on too much responsibility, or become codependent in relationships. Guilt can look like any of these scenarios:

"Maybe I'm the reason my parents aren't happy. I need to do better, be better."

"If I was more lovable, maybe my sister wouldn't hit me every night and she'd be happy to spend time with me."

"I need to help my mom because my father doesn't treat her right."

"I'm okay if you're okay, so I'm going to do whatever I can to make sure you're okay."

Guilt is bred from difficult life events that lead a person to believe they are responsible for how others feel. Of course, we should have a healthy way to own guilt when we are at fault. The guilt described here is guilt that is created by an unhealthy attachment to another, and taking on unnecessary responsibility. This kind of guilt is a breeding ground for a host of toxic emotions such as anger, resentment, denial, rebellion, feeling out of control, and shame. Young minds and hearts cannot process the emotions of others besides the basic level of love, sorrow, disappointment, and fear. So they learn to carry the pain or grief of others with them until guilt becomes a part of their emotional imprint.

Using the list on the following page, write the words in your journal that you have most experienced over the course of your life when you felt imbalanced. This will help you understand if your primary source of toxic emotion stems from a place of shame or guilt, or a combination of both.

- Lack of ambition
- Control issues
- Digestive disorders
- Loneliness
- Fibromyalgia
- Addiction
- Need for power
- Stubbornness
- Passivity
- Selfishness
- Feeling unworthy
- Low stamina
- Aggression
- Lack of confidence
- Defensiveness
- Self-criticism
- Sarcasm
- Need to dominate
- Obsessive compulsive disorder
- Eating disorders
- Helplessness
- Shaming self or others
- Type A personality
- Emotional outbursts
- Entitlement issues
- Widening of hips

- Depression
- Unproductivity
- Low back pain
- Jealousy
- Fear
- Lack of libido
- Adrenal fatigue
- Bloating
- Intimacy issues
- Codependency
- Addiction to food or sex
- Excess fat
- Fluid retention
- Lack of creativity
- Moodiness or stuck emotions
- Abnormal bowel function
- Sexual obsession
- Feeling detached
- Reproductive issues
- Urinary or kidney problems
- Inability to maintain relationships
- Lymphatic issues
- Tightness in hips or knees
- Apathy

If you chose more descriptors from the list on the left, your predominant emotional imprint is likely based on shame. If you chose more from the right, your imprint is based more in guilt. It is very common for you to have a combination of both.

If shame is the most toxic emotion stemming from your core wound, you may feel unsafe or unworthy in intimate or close relationships. Shame blocks a healthy sense of self, a vital life flow of productivity, and the ability to have healthy relationships and experiences, while guilt is toxic to passion, connection, and creativity.

However shame and guilt are experienced, they are often the foundation for self-loathing and self-sabotage. Born from shame and guilt are insecurities, lack of ambition, and fear of intimacy and/or relationships—all low vibrational frequencies that feel terrible. Shame and guilt may be keeping you from going after a new job or living the life you want because you can't abandon the familiar energy imprint you've created or fear that you'll be forced out of this sense of familiarity.

When you don't feel good or worthy enough, it's hard to strive for something better, much less live your dreams. Typically, people with an abundance of shame and guilt are unable to self-identify or maintain a good feeling (higher vibration) long enough to have a day without anxiety or panic. Ultimately, we fear that we are the problem. We believe no one will love and attend to us, or if we had only been (fill in the blank), then life would be better. This sets up a guilty conscience that many people are unable to identify.

Humans are imperfect beings and make mistakes. Everyone says that as if they "know," but knowing and accepting are very different. If you accept the part of yourself that isn't perfect, you don't have to beat yourself up over shortcomings. You need to come to your truth and understand how your toxic emotions developed. If you grew up believing that you were the reason for someone else's feelings, or believed that you were bad, you will do whatever you can to avoid more shame or guilt. It's a survival skill. It's also an excuse to keep you from realizing your dreams or living a satisfying life.

If you are mindful and aligned with your soul, it will be possible to follow your moral guidelines, and release the need to follow another's idea of who you should be. That's why this work of owning and getting on your own path is important. If you fail to release the toxic emotions that you developed or inherited, you will not be free to grow and become stronger. Your life mission is not to carry forward the negative emotional patterns of your past or your ancestry, but to learn how to love, evolve, and rise to meet your highest self.

The amount of emotional maturity this requires is huge, so you can add maturity to your list of positive attributes just by attempting this kind of work. Keep in mind that owning your feelings and not blaming others does not mean that you agree with the behavior of others or the way you were treated. It means that you recognize and acknowledge your feelings, whatever they are, and it is up to you to work through them and make change.

Toxic emotions don't happen overnight. They are accumulated over time and based on tons of emotional exchanges. Everything you do has a purpose and a value, whether you realize it or not. After you establish your truth from your story in the following chapter, you'll come to find the value and purpose of your choices. You can't change history, but as you learn about emotional and energetic imprints, you'll begin to see how unprocessed toxic emotions have held you back from some of life's greatest moments.

Chapter 2
Understand Your Emotional Imprints

EMOTIONAL imprints are developed early in life. They are typically based on how we were treated by others, what we observed in our environment, and how we emotionally interpreted these behaviors. Think of emotional imprints as a veil of energy cords woven together like fabric that lives within and around your body.

Your body has connective tissues that keep its diverse physical systems running smoothly. Your thoughts, emotions, and energy are also systems that retain memories of external experiences. This data collection starts when we are infants and evolves and continues well into adulthood. We develop an understanding of the roles that people play in our lives as well as an understanding of our self-worth. We create beliefs based on these roles, which then generate emotional responses. These emotional responses embed deep into our belief system, and imprint into our mental and emotional functioning system.

Imprints are important to understand because they influence how we operate and interpret life, and how we perceive our own identity. Our emotional imprints not only dictate how we understand relationships, but also serve as the system of judgment for ourselves and others. When you understand how much of your current feelings are associated with the emotional energetic imprints of your past, you can then create new imprints that are supportive, informative, and transformative.

Like fingerprints and snowflakes, each emotional imprint is completely unique. Your specific environment and the people in it combined with your distinct personality and emotional sensitivities created the unique design of your imprint. Because we are individuals, our struggle to be understood or heal can make us feel very alone, but the impact of our unique imprints has similar consequences, so we can all share resources to heal.

Your expectations of people are dependent on the expectations you came to trust as developed by the beliefs that imprinted in your mind-emotion-energy body. All of this is normal. Not to be judged, but understood. In your young developmental years, every negative experience made an impact and rendered you with a certain belief or feeling (the imprint). As you relate these interpretations to the beliefs you hold about yourself, you'll see how deeply these imprints affect the psyche and your emotional capacity to have relationships with others.

For example, if Dad was often drunk and treated you poorly while inebriated, you may have a belief that you are not worthy of love (specifically by men) on a day-to-day basis. This belief was built on layers of information absorbed by all of your senses over the years in relation to time spent with your father. Although your mind can rationalize the impact now, an emotional imprint had already developed in childhood from feeling scared, alone, or ignored around the prominent male figure in your young life. It may have also left a mental belief that alcohol is dangerous, or worse, an emotional imprint that you aren't worth more than the substance of alcohol. As a child, you may have become emotionally confused (not knowing when Dad was sober or when you were going to be treated better), codependent (believing that your own happiness depends on the happiness of others), or lonely.

Children do not often blame their parents for poor treatment; they blame themselves. This self-blame sets the stage for chronic shame, guilt, and lack of positive identity. Children learn who they are and what value they have to the world by observing actions, words, and behaviors from the people around them. You may have a false belief that you are not worthy or truly seen. This isn't a fact. What is factual is that the person who instilled this false belief in you had emotional wounds and limitations that made them unable to see you, validate you, encourage you, or give you the childhood nurturing that you needed.

We interpret life by witnessing our environment. If you benefited from a healthy environment filled with emotional and mental support, you have a very different experience from a person who didn't. Children who feel denied or unable to measure up to certain standards have an extremely hard time feeling accepted and loved.

Children subconsciously take on too much responsibility for the happiness and well-being of others. We want Mom or Dad (or Brother/Sister) to be all right, because we love them and want them to be happy. We also strive to get the love we need. Our desire to help comes from a loving and innocent place, but ultimately there is a need to survive.

The "if they're okay, I'll be okay" mentality can easily set the stage for attachment issues, codependency, enmeshment, and other unhealthy relational behaviors. It is not appropriate for a child to feel responsible for anyone's needs outside of the healthy exchange of loving and being loved. Childhood is the time when we learn what is "right" and "wrong" and how to be responsible for our words and actions. But a child who takes on adult responsibilities cannot process the depth of what is at play. Children should not counsel their parents, or be their primary comfort or support system. Children need to feel safe and be loved in order to develop into mature emotional beings. Children crave discipline, learning, and healthy boundaries.

Because the reality of a child's situation is all they know, it can become normal to accept unhealthy behaviors. If children grow up experiencing screaming matches, hitting, neglect, or substance addiction issues, it is all they know. It's their reality. Many adults say that their childhoods seemed normal because that's the way the household typically functioned. Many of those same adults experienced abuse and/or trauma within the greater family system or community at large.

Even if your family was free of deeper dysfunctions such as abuse or neglect, you may have been affected by more subtle discomforts such as disapproving glances, emotional manipulation, energetic distancing, unrealistic expectations, or unsettling drama. The mental impact of these kinds of subtleties can leave a lasting effect, but identifying our emotional imprints and applying the AAA Method can make it possible to change your perspective, emotional imprint, and reality.

It's common to categorize your emotions as either bad or good. That's what our minds do. Exploring our imprints and vibrational frequencies can help us learn to recognize how and why we do this so we can operate from a different understanding. Although you may feel bad and want to feel better, it doesn't mean that something is wrong with you or you aren't good enough. Try to know when this mental judgment happens and reframe the thought by tapping into the emotion.

Emotions can teach us about our patterns, experiences, and where we are imbalanced. The key is to fully process our emotions and allow them to filter through a healthier lens. By applying tools to reset and find our center, we can shift our vibration higher and experience more internal ease and freedom. For example, too often anger and fear get bad raps. While certainly not enjoyed or encouraged, anger and fear are valid emotions that are needed in certain times, and they deserve our understanding. The ability to attend and understand creates connection to self, and empathy that can be extended to others who are also dealing with anger or fear.

Our emotions are palpable, each emotion having its own frequency, and part of the intensity of emotions is the fluctuation of those frequencies. When we understand how and when imprints were formed, and work to raise our vibration into a healthier state, we can become more aware and sensitive to our needs. If we can determine if the frequency is serving us well or keeping us addicted to negative patterns, we can learn to take action in order to retune and sustain the frequency for a better life experience. It's exciting stuff!

Challenges in Healing

It is human nature to live in packs, so lack of connection or complete isolation can have a detrimental effect on the psyche and physical and emotional health of an individual. One of the biggest challenges as we heal is to step outside the energy matrix of the family. Each system has its own energy and imprint, and to heal and grow means that we begin to operate differently, which may impact the way we feel in relation to the unit.

In our self-growth journey there is often a subliminal fear of abandoning old belief systems. If you are tied to certain belief systems within your family such as limited abundance, self-insecurities, or shame in sexuality, it can be terrifying to feel like you are separating from them as you evolve and heal. Even though you are not physically leaving your family, when you begin to change (mentally, emotionally, or energetically), this will be felt by the others, leading to an overall vibrational shift in the family unit.

No matter how bad our feelings may be, there is an underlying fear that if we abandon those feelings, we will no longer have support from and connection with our loved ones. It makes creating new emotional imprints difficult. Your current imprints, woven together, create a comfort zone. A new imprint creates a different relationship pattern to those around you, but it should not sever the bond of love or affection.

Another difficult aspect of healing is the urge to defend our parents or caregivers. The love you have for your parents is a bond that is stronger than most any wrongdoing. Although we do not want to blame them any longer, we also do not need to make excuses or justifications for their behavior. This only serves to keep the pain cycle activated, trapping in our shame, fear, or guilt. We can learn to accept our love for them while also acknowledging how we were hurt by their behavior or lack thereof. And while we are not blaming in our self-care journey, we also should not protect or defend others. That only diminishes the impact that was left on our psyches and emotional health.

Only when we consciously employ a process of being open and honest about how others treated us can we make progress. It's common to get stuck trying to unravel the "why" behind their actions, or the good intentions that we believed existed. Let's stop making excuses for not getting the nurturing that we needed and move toward acceptance of that fact. It doesn't make your parents bad people. For this healing work, I suggest keeping the focus on *you*. Acknowledge the shame, guilt, or fear that you experienced, accept those feelings as real (even if someone did the best they could), and apply new action to heal the pains that suffocate you. Remember, if our focus is on the other, we relinquish our power to them. It's time to bring the focus back to self, apply the knowledge that you now have, and accept the weight of your burdens.

Although you may partially realize that your childhood affected your adulthood, it's important to understand its long-term ramifications. If you had negative childhood experiences, you may feel isolated in your current situation, or not good enough to be in a loving relationship. You may be on edge and unsure what to expect day to day, while keeping people at arm's length so they don't get too close to you. You may not know what nontoxic, consistent intimacy is—how could you if you didn't experience it? The longing for attention and closeness is there, but you may be caught in the energetic web of a negative imprint that keeps you from having a healthier experience. And like most patterns, we repeatedly find ourselves reverting back to the same negative experiences. Why?

Because we become addicted to pain.

Addiction sounds harsh, but emotional addiction is real and needs to be addressed to break free. Our pain points are so ingrained in our emotional systems and mental beliefs that they are absorbed in our energy fields. This cycle is very hard to break. Below we will look at the link of addictions to emotions and how we experience pleasure from our pain.

It's also not surprising if you are attracted to relationships or situations with people who "make you feel" similar to the first person who caused you shame or pain. Even if the situations are not the same, you are still left *feeling* the same. This is a critical distinction. Subconsciously, we seek to recreate the emotional vibrations that are attached to our imprint. Therefore, we attract people into our lives that leave us with this same feeling. It's not a relationship chosen consciously. Let's delve into why this feeling became a certain vibration within you that helped create and attract most every other experience in your life. Because your imprint is unique to you, it is your personal responsibility to be aware of your patterns.

I invite you to pause for a moment. Close your eyes and recognize the awareness deep in your body. Become present. Allow yourself to bring forward the general memory of what it felt like to be a child. Don't judge it. For now, just feel it. Think of all the people, the nights at home, the mornings, the weekends, the dinners, your bedroom. Just allow yourself to connect to the memories that formed your childhood and notice how those memories make you feel. Sit with it for a moment, envisioning the web of emotions that are within you and that form your energetic field. When you open your eyes, jot down your experience. Be clear about the emotions that you felt, or beliefs and memories that passed through your mind. Try not to filter. We'll come back to this and use that information.

Let's focus now on your parents. They are main characters in your story. As such, they are critical elements to your imprint. Everything you learned came from watching, interacting with, and sensing how life operates in relationship to these characters. While with your parents or caregivers, you developed beliefs about everything from relationships and survival, to behaviors and expectations. These formative beliefs stemmed from your relational patterns with your parents or caregivers. You began to understand the meaning of connection, and formed overall judgments of people, things, and the world.

Not only were you learning *about* these things, each interaction or person you witnessed "made you *feel*" a certain way. Every experience had a strong impact along with a strong memory (even if you are not consciously aware of it), which created an emotional belief system that you are likely still operating from today. It is critical to fully understand the role of emotional imprints to better understand how you have been reliving these patterns. The memory of each experience, coupled with the emotions felt throughout the body, creates an overall energy sensation deep in our cells. As we mature, these sensations may seem subtle, but become activated through the subconscious and memory tissue as a reaction to most all experiences.

We too often live our adult lives through the operating system of our old imprints, and it doesn't work anymore. Your higher self is awakening and knows that something needs to change. You are tired of feeling this way, which might be why you are reading this book. Your lower vibration patterning doesn't align with your highest vibrational potential. This is why most people seek self-care work. They have experienced the same low-grade discomfort, or perhaps a deep sense of self-loathing, or had bad relationships for too long. Nothing seems to fix it. They feel stuck and want to break free.

Many of my clients who are successful, mature, highly functioning adults tell me that inside, they feel like scared, pained children. They have lost sight of their own realities or truth—no matter what barometers of success prove otherwise. They feel chronically sad, disappointed, or unable to feel peace. These are highly intelligent folks flummoxed by their insecurities. It's more common than you think.

Our imprints are such a powerful force that it is common to feel magnetized to them, sucked back to any negative vibration that is held in our being. It's vitally important to continue strengthening yourself through healing in order to create new, healthy vibrations that can lead to life-changing beliefs. I know you would like a quick fix or magic bullet, but working through these chapters and applying the AAA Method will help give you the support you need. You are already in the process of shifting.

It's frustrating to do years of therapy or healing work, only to see patterns repeat and emotions resurface. In fact, your frustration is a sign that you are targeting your core wounds and making progress. This method doesn't ask you to abandon that critical path to your overall growth. It provides additional perspective to your imprints, but don't expect them to just go away in one fell swoop.

Although similar to traditional therapy that asks us to look at our family history and identify unhealthy patterns or childhood wounds, the AAA Method examines the imprints created and how they impact our perceptions of the world so that we can rebuild a new system in our lives now. Particularly why we are magnetized back to our imprints, even when negative, and how imprints dominate our sense of worth, expectations of others, and relationships to others and self.

Building New Imprints

If you want a different experience, to rise up from the self-sabotage, you have to settle the conflict within you. This conflict comes about from being stuck in limited beliefs rather than living in your authenticity and believing in the power of your reality and potential.

How do we change and build new imprints?

AAA Method

Acknowledgment (consciously recognize the false beliefs and feelings created by our early childhood experience).

Acceptance (make peace with the feelings and false beliefs that formed).

Action (take a step toward our higher self, including re-parenting our inner child, applying compassion, and self-love).

Building new imprints requires utilizing this method at the ready. Be aware that developing new patterns will take some internal heavy lifting. This means recognizing your imprints and vibrations on the daily and using the AAA Method to create change. It doesn't just happen overnight, but applied over time you will notice a substantial difference.

Vibrations

Why do we care about vibrations when talking about toxic emotions? Simply put, higher vibrations support the growth of self-actualization and emotional and mental wellness. Toxic emotions cannot live or breed in the frequency of higher vibrations. Learning to raise your vibration is key to expansion and personal growth. Would you like some good vibrations? Don't we all. Nothing better than feeling light, positive, and high on the world. Good feels good. But if we're used to feeling bad, good can be hard to hold on to. How do we make it last?

Understanding that emotions create certain vibrations and that you can control your emotions is a game changer. You don't have to be a mystic to understand. To raise your vibration is to acknowledge that energy exists, and that your thoughts, feelings, and physical body create energy depending on the environment and how you experience situations.

The depth of information regarding emotional frequencies is fascinating. There are specific measuring tools that read the frequency of the human body, your brain, heartbeat, and vocal tone. The Scale of Positive and Negative Experience (SPANE) is one of the most respected and referenced studies that measures the positive and negative effects of emotional vibrations.

Emotional frequency is the vibration with which each emotion resonates. We feel emotional frequencies in every moment of every day. Remember, every thought has a feeling associated with it, and every feeling has a thought. The next page includes some examples that pull us to a lower vibration:

34

- Chronic negative mentality
- Addictive emotional patterns
- Unhealthy relationships
- Anger, resentment, jealousy, revenge, shame, guilt
- Chemical drugs
- Excessive natural intoxicators (wine, tobacco, coffee)
- Unhealthy processed foods
- Self-criticism
- Unprocessed emotions
- Being judgmental of self or others
- Toxic household cleaning products
- Chemically laden foods
- Exposure to electromagnetic frequency
- Blaming others for our feelings
- Dishonesty
- Taking things that aren't ours

Below are some examples that pull us to a higher vibration.
- Connection to nature
- Healthy, natural foods and herbs
- Practicing being mindful and present
- High-vibe music
- Sunlight
- Self-love
- Gratitude
- Connection to spirit
- Compassion
- Meditation and breath work
- Giving back to others
- Surrounding yourself with beauty
- Laughter
- Exercise
- Prayer

- Acts of kindness and generosity
- Eliminating toxic foods and substances from the body

The higher the vibrational frequency, the more energy or life force you will experience in your cells. Feelings such as happiness, bliss, and connection have a certain frequency that will make you feel healthier, lighter, and more centered in your highest self. Feelings such as rage, fear, or resentment emit lower frequencies that may feel heavy, sludgy, or dark. Like all forms of energy, emotional energy expands and contracts depending on the frequency it has. Joy and laughter are expansive energies, while shame and scowling are constrictive energies.

When you are vibrating at a higher frequency that supports feelings of peace, joy, love, and contentment, you are better able to manage difficult emotions, and the likelihood of feeling high levels of bodily pains is lower. Whereas, when you are vibrating at a lower frequency that supports feelings of anger, sadness, self-loathing, or guilt, it is more difficult to process challenging experiences and emotions, and you may experience higher levels of bodily pain.

AAA Method

Acknowledge that energy exists and you can control your energy according to your thoughts, feelings, and environment.

Accept the thoughts and feelings that are within you. Acceptance makes way for action. If we do not accept, our actions will be based on addiction to our imprints instead of healing and raising our vibration.

Act by taking micro-steps that are manageable, achievable, and easy to repeat to raise and sustain your vibration.

Basically, what you emit is a reflection of how you feel. What you emit is also what you attract. The vibration level that you carry will resonate with the vibration level of someone or something else, and soon you'll find yourself playing out your patterns together.

It never ceases to amaze me that even in my work, I attract new clients going through similar situations as existing clients. And sometimes both are parallel to a previous or current personal scenario. It's as if I had a menu on my services offering "the narcissist-codependent dance" and people are flocking to it, without even realizing its ingredients. They don't have to. The frequency I was putting out on the topic was exploding into the cosmic waves and people who resonate at that level recognize the vibe and reach out. That's the way it works. We call it amazing, magical, unreal, the craziest thing. It's energy.

You can feel energy, even if you aren't trying to feel it. The more you tap into the subtle awareness of energy, the more you become attuned to your higher self. Some people feel it as a palpable charge, others sense it, and some claim to see it. Regardless, it's important to be clear on what energy feels like in our emotional bodies so that we can better identify our specific vibrational frequency.

Some people may claim that they don't feel anything. They can't sense their emotional bodies or energy. That's okay. It's common to experience a block in our emotional connection if we are dissociated, have extreme stress, or feel unsupported. As you move through the AAA Method and practice, you will become more sensitive. First, you have to become grounded and learn to trust yourself in this moment.

Have you ever been in a home or office and didn't like the vibe? Maybe it felt dark, heavy, or frenetic. It may be difficult to say exactly what it felt like, but you know it didn't feel good. That's an example of what it feels like when outside energies are not aligned with your own. In this situation, the vibe in the office was vibrating lower than your current vibrational frequency. Remember, there is no judgment; just because it didn't feel good doesn't mean your energy is better or that another's energy is worse. The energies just didn't match. Sometimes we can feel when the energy is lower than ours, which makes us feel less good, and we call it bad. But let's step into the empowering position and acknowledge that the energy isn't a match.

Take the example of using public transportation in a city. You board and sit or stand next to someone because space is limited. If you feel uncomfortable, threatened, or even have a physical response like feeling hot or sticky, this person's vibration is not a match for you. The energy vibration is emitting a frequency that is disturbing to you. Maybe it reminds you of energy frequencies during times of actual threat or harm. Maybe it resembles your own frequency at times when you've been self-sabotaging or self-loathing. You know in your body that this lower vibration doesn't feel good.

On the other hand, perhaps you sat next to someone and felt comfortable, safe, and at ease. This person may have matched your current vibration or carried a familiar one matching that of an experience you had with a friend or grandparent. We sense energy and vibrational frequencies every moment of every day. We sense it with people, spaces, animals, crystals, plants, homes—everything. We sense it in natural environments, the beach, the desert, the mountains, or a tree-lined country road. Energy is everywhere, and without thinking much about it, we gravitate toward the energy that most aligns with us as we crave to bring ourselves to a place of familiarity and balance.

Now, here's what's tricky about balance. What seems like balance isn't always healthy balance. As we know, if we are operating from our original emotional imprints, we may find comfort in situations and with people who are aligned with our wounded self, rather than our higher self. Balancing these imprints would continue a cycle of addiction to pain, so we should be careful when thinking about balance. If we are working on shifting and building better relationships, it's beneficial to acknowledge when we're pulling from our emotional imprints (our story), or from the place of raising our vibration (some may call this our higher self, our new reality).

Let's look at the vibrational difference between greasy fast food and fresh organic vegetables. Calories, fat, and nutritional content aside, on a vibrational level the span is quite great. Greasy fast food has a lower frequency. If you currently crave and find the most comfort in fast food, you are likely operating from a lower vibrational level. No judgment here. We all experience this kind of pull and craving—that's why they call it comfort food. But someone operating from a higher vibrational level might call an organic peach comfort food. This person may have been taught to love in a way that fed the body optimally, and their wounded vibrational patterns may show up somewhere else.

When considering vibration, it gets interesting when we look at our choices and even our self-expression in clothes and material things. Once we tap into the vibrational feelings in our bodies and give that vibration acknowledgment, we can use the AAA Method to more easily attune to a higher frequency. Intentional, mindful thinking on its own has a high frequency, so applying that will help you vibrate higher.

Determining Your Vibrational Baseline

Let's figure out what your vibrational baseline is according to your beliefs. Remember, your vibrational baseline correlates to your emotional imprints developed at a young age, so you may have a variety of frequencies surrounding different situations.

To start, let's agree that there is no judgment in this practice. I find that no matter how many times I say this, many people's first response is self-criticism. Going back to the shame response we discussed on page 17, you may feel like a wreck, but that isn't a feeling—what you are feeling is a lower vibration attached to your core wound. Shame, guilt, fear, sadness . . . these feelings are here to teach you. Your higher self has brought you here to learn to vibe up and feel whole.

For the purposes of this book, we will focus on the average baseline number to give you something tangible to work with as you move forward. But you can apply the process of this work to any kind of difficult emotion or lower frequency that you have.

We'll use a simple 1–10 scale to note your vibration. A vibration of one would be a feeling that is low, slow, dense, fearful, heavy, weak, traumatic, sad, angry, terrified, or like there is a void within you. A vibration of five would be a feeling of mediocrity, okay-ness, emotional tolerance, mild trauma, despondence, a "just live with it" attitude, or moderate negativity. This vibration has a partial block to love, aspirations, beauty, and joy. A vibration of ten would be feelings of lightness, freedom, support, love, security, enlightenment, safety, and total bliss. This vibration is in complete alignment with your highest self. You may be an angel and spontaneously evaporate at any moment!

Before you get set on the number, remember that this work isn't about negating the good in your life. That said, even if you experienced an upbeat, hopeful, loving, and fun childhood that left you with a vibrational feeling of eight, I want you to factor in what was *really* going on around you. If you felt like an eight in your thoughts or perceived reality, but were bullied by your brother, or your mom was aggressive and verbally abusive, or you were alone at home most of the time, your average number may actually be a six. This scale of vibration isn't about what you think of yourself or another person at the lowest of times or even the best of times in your childhood. It is strictly a vibrational frequency attached to emotion.

Even though a vibration of one may feel low, bad, or less than, this doesn't mean that you or anyone is low, bad, or less than. It's just a number to help us uncover our true feelings. Judgment only keeps us in the cycle of blame or feeling shame, so we are moving beyond that. If we don't do the work to uncover our true feelings, we won't have an accurate vibrational baseline from which to work. Assistance from friends, safe family members, therapists, and healers may offer support to reflect back the truth of what you may not be able to recall.

Close your eyes and get in touch with that same feeling you tapped into on page 31 that has trailed you since you were a child. Recognize the good feelings, the difficult ones, and the overall emotional imprint that you feel around your energy.

On an instinctual, guttural level, what number would you ascribe to your average, overall vibrational frequency when remembering your general feeling as a child? Write that number down, and note the people and circumstances that "made you feel" that way.

_____

_____

_____

What number would you ascribe to your lowest vibrational frequency as a child? Write that number down, and note the people and circumstances that "made you feel" that way.

_____

_____

_____

What number would you ascribe to your highest vibrational frequency as a child? Write that number down, and note the people and circumstances that "made you feel" that way.

_____

_____

_____

Your average vibrational baseline is likely the middle number between your lowest and highest vibrational frequencies, but sometimes we have an average that doesn't exactly measure that way. This may be the result of a particular trauma that had a deep impact and created a low vibration for many years, but our memory aside from that trauma elicits a higher feeling. Other factors that could skew our overall number include selective memory, denial, dissociation, and/or using coping mechanisms, which may have felt healthier at the time than they actually were.

Because you are reading this book and have experienced difficult relationships and emotions, it's likely that your baseline average is a six or under. Many who struggle with toxic emotions of shame, guilt, fear, abandonment, resentment, or other long-held pain hover in the realm of 1–5. For most people, it's useful to reference experiences between the ages of two to thirteen years old. If you are unable to remember that far back, or had difficult experiences later in your teens, reflect back on ages thirteen to eighteen.

During childhood, if you regularly felt fearful, abandoned, unloved, scared, invisible, worthless, guilty, or were abused or manipulated, your vibrational baseline may be closer to a two or three. If your childhood was pleasant and your needs were met but either or both of your parents were emotionally or physically absent, your number may fall between a five or seven. If life felt lousy in general but you had a loving grandmother, for example, it doesn't qualify for a higher score. Instead, recognize your relationship with her as its own imprint with a varying vibrational baseline, or as your highest vibrational imprint.

Vibration scoring is personal. It's unique to you and you do not need to defend or justify your number. Just make sure it resonates with your true feelings. Your vibrational baselines will guide you to consciously look at the behaviors, relationships, and life experiences to which you have been attracted or those that have been attracted to you. If your average emotional imprint resonates with a four vibration, this means that until you step on the path of conscious healing, you will likely attract people and experiences that allow you to keep feeling like a four.

Our emotional imprints are hard to break, but very possible with the AAA Method. Reverting back to the frequency of your emotional imprint is like an addiction. It doesn't mean that you are happy or feel good in your vibrational pattern. It is just what you know and where you have resonated for so long, that now it is part of you. This familiar energy guides your behaviors and leaves you with a belief that you are forever caught in this defeatist cycle. But you are not.

Some therapists ask their clients to examine their relationships with their parents to better understand why they have relationships with certain mates and friends. We sometimes find people who treat us like one of our parents treated us. It's typically the parent with whom we had the most issues, as we attempt to heal our wounds in association with them. Because cognitive therapy only affects the mind and beliefs, I believe we have to go even deeper and effect change in our emotional and energetic frequencies.

We attract people who are not the same as our parent, but who allow us to *feel* the same emotional frequency as that parent. For example, it's not necessary to attract someone like your father to heal the difficult relationship you had with him. If he was abusive, dismissive, or emotionally unavailable, and you felt lonely, misunderstood, or undervalued (let's call that a three), you may attract someone who has different qualities but still brings out the same feelings of loneliness, etc. Or you may attract someone completely opposite who is nurturing and present (resisting the familiar three vibration in your personal life), in which case you may have other patterns such as addiction or unhealthy friendships that bring you to feel the vibration of a three. Somewhere in your personal life, the pattern of a three vibration will manifest.

We cannot rely on someone else to elevate our own emotional well-being. If we cannot sustain a higher feeling or vibration on our own, we will not be able to sustain it within a relationship with someone who is attempting to make us feel better, so it's important to keep reminding ourselves to release blame and focus on healing.

The Roller Coaster of Addiction

Your vibrational baseline isn't the same in all scenarios. We often create cycles and patterns depending on different types of relationships and circumstances. Most of us have a vibrational pattern that if illustrated would look like a ride on a roller coaster. Have you had a roller-coaster experience with a personal or intimate relationship?

An emotional roller coaster swings us up and down with highs and lows. The good times are great, and the bad times are terrible, causing emotional whiplash as the toxicity of it all is unleashed. Being on an up-and-down ride matches many of our imprints and addictions, as we reach for higher vibrational experiences, and then crash down and experience a low. That low can feel so bad, even lower than your baseline low, which creates pain that can trigger self-sabotaging patterns or detrimental behaviors. In recovery we strive to come back to our baseline before being able to apply healing strategies to raise our vibration.

When we act out our emotional addictions we find that the peaks are actually pain points just as much as the dips are pain points. We are addicted to the entire cycle and the expectation that we will eventually return to our "comfort" level of pain. The higher the peak, the harder the fall. Both feed the same addiction to pain.

What we should aim for is to close the gap between the peak and the dip. That doesn't mean trying to limit high points in our lives. It means focusing on raising our vibrations to a level through positive micro-steps that can be sustained with daily self-growth. Then, we don't see the highs as a form of self-sabotage. The more emotionally attuned we are to health, the more regularly we feel balanced and can integrate the peak experience, instead of reverting back to the addiction to pain.

Sometimes balance feels boring and addictions feel exciting. I get that. But healthy balance that is full of awareness, acceptance, joy, and peace is more exciting than any toxic hit of emotion you could ever feel. There's a mantra I use in my life and in my work that can help free us from our addictive nature.

"I'm addicted to feeling bad. I'm committed to feeling good."
Emotional addiction is real. Not only do we crave and hold on to
familiar emotional patterns, we also put great effort into winning the
affection of others. Seeking validation is part of an addictive pattern.
These addictions keep us stuck in our lower vibrational imprints (and
toxic emotions), as we look to others to identify our worth.

If you struggle with addiction, (and we all do because we all have
emotionally addictive patterns), your addiction keeps you attached to
the pain of your vibrational frequency. You can even think of your
vibrational baseline as an addiction, as addictive feelings and patterns
of pain emerge within relationships all the time. Pain can not only feel
easy or familiar, it can also resonate a particular frequency that is alluring. When we are too far away from our baseline, especially in the positive sense, we start craving the feeling of our known pain, and we begin
self-sabotaging behaviors. People use various kinds of self-sabotage to
control pain but simultaneously find comfort within that pain.

I was in a difficult relationship. It would be easy for me to diagnose the other person with a popular personality disorder and blame
him for my misery. But, because I broke up with blame, I'm going to
tell you about my experience in this relationship pattern.

My history is to attract unavailable men. Emotionally unavailable,
mentally unavailable, physically unavailable—I was never picky with
the type, so long as I was (subconsciously) sure that I wouldn't get my
needs met. The relationship wasn't all bad. There were many times of
laughs, deep connection, and new experiences. But when it was bad, it
was really bad. He displayed his rage with verbal attacks and shouting.
All-night fights ended with me in tears. I even slept in my car on occa-
sion to escape. There were weeks with no communication, and years
of trying to understand him. I would try to do better so that he would
treat me better. I tried to fix him, and I walked on eggshells. At times
I was afraid of being physically hurt. The relationship "made me feel"
less than, abandoned, insecure, guilty, and ashamed.

Please read what I'm about to say with a renewed understanding of emotional imprints and energy: I was seeking to relive all of

those emotions and experiences. Not consciously, but subconsciously. Energetically. Those terrible feelings and experiences allowed me to stay hooked to the negative beliefs and toxic emotions I felt and addicted to my own pain. He and that relationship "made me feel" the same negative beliefs and toxic emotions I harbored within myself and the same addiction to pain. I would never suggest that this is the kind of relationship I consciously sought, but because I was stuck in a negative pattern, it's the only relationship that worked with my vibration.

Let's say I was vibrating at a four in regard to intimate relationships at that time. I was starving for affection and desperate to be nurtured in ways I didn't receive as a young person. I'd say some of those feelings from my childhood had me feeling like a two. Yet, I also knew there was a better way. I'd seen it and read about it and felt in my soul that I was capable of healthier love. The yearning to experience real love felt like I could have an eight experience. My higher self knew it, but my dense human self wasn't yet ready to accept it.

In this case, I chose a man who initially I found attractive. I felt like the possibility of an eight was there for sure. He was funny. (Eight.) He was smart. (Eight.) He was sensitive and intuitive in interesting ways. (Seven.) We shared in mutual work and creativity. (Nine.) But he was also hurt and angry, which when on display felt like a two. Full of shame. (Three.) Manipulative. (Two.) Didn't know how to be emotionally vulnerable. (Three.) Wasn't reliable. (Two.) Selfish. (Three.)

Ascribing numbers to people and emotional issues may seem like judgment. It's not. I'm not rating another person's humanity. These are the vibrational numbers I felt in this relationship, and are merely a marker of my own emotional and energetic frequency. While in the relationship I would experience highs and feel like an eight. And I also experienced many lows that felt like a two. As you see, the swing between these two levels held me to an average of 4.5, which was near my baseline emotional imprint.

I was on a roller coaster.

What's interesting about an emotional roller coaster is that most people think they are seeking the high because it "feels" good. We know the high is temporary and the higher we go, the lower we will fall. In regard to vibrations and our addiction to them, we actually seek the low. The low *is* the high. The low is what feeds and traps us to our emotional imprint comfort zone. The low confirms we aren't good enough and don't deserve to be happy.

Similar to drugs, the low is what keeps us addicted. If we didn't have the low, be it a hard day, stress that needs to be released, pain that needs attention, or sleepless nights—we wouldn't need the high. To make the ride smoother and close the gap between highs and lows, use the AAA Method:

AAA Method

Acknowledge what you're feeling—good, too good, or bad.

Accept that you're seeking a high, to distract you from your low; only to take you back to chasing a high.

Act by stabilizing your emotions and taking small micro-steps to sustain a vibration that feels somewhat higher than your baseline.

Many of us would like to move from 0–100. We hope for a spontaneous miracle to help us forget the negative place we came from so that we can move into a new territory of green grass and daisies. This is why the "letting go" theory is so popular. It supports the idea that if we can just move on, our life will change and we will be free. But it doesn't work that way. Building a new imprint doesn't mean killing off your old self. It means fully acknowledging and accepting who you are with conscious thought and taking action to rebuild from a place of acknowledgment and acceptance.

When you acknowledge how often you crave a feeling or experience that will take you way up or way down, you gain better control of your addictions. Some of us have this swing throughout every day, while others may experience it monthly or even yearly. When you're in control, you can begin to follow through with acceptance and action.

Food, again, is a good example. You *know* that a box of chocolate chip cookies is not good for you and that eating the entire box will make you feel bad. When you're in control, you can stop at one or two. That's a balanced emotional day. When you're out of control and need a hit, you eat the whole thing. What you're really doing is seeking the low that is associated with your pain points. Addiction to food is a source of self-sabotage. For many, it's easier to control something tangible that affects how we feel physically than to deal with emotional pain.

Act to Heal

The action element is key to changing our emotional imprints and vibrational frequencies. Some action may, in fact, be large decisions or behavioral modifications that will alter your entire life, but most helpful in the scope of healing are what I call micro-steps. They will allow you to transition to a slightly higher vibrational feeling that you can sustain. To stop the cycle of feeding addiction patterns and reverting back to negative imprints, the ability to sustain a higher frequency is vital. Over time, micro-steps create a strong foundation for positive change.

One of the problems we have with making change and healing is that we become overwhelmed. We take on more than we can handle, hoping for big change now. The urge is to turn in your old life and start anew. I encourage you to find hope in the resurrection, rising up from where you came, not extinguishing your past altogether. Overwhelm is a distraction to real change.

Healing doesn't happen all at once. It's not about creating a new life, it's about co-creating this moment with new meaning. If you were to paint a picture of a house on a farm, you wouldn't throw 10 colors of paint at the canvas all at once and hope for a house to appear. You would take it one brush stroke at a time, creating, then recreating, enhancing lines, shadowing, giving texture, and blending, until at some point you'd step back and see a house on a farm. The final product is like magic, but the process is a lot of hard work.

Being overwhelmed comes from knowing we feel like x, we desire to feel like z, and subconsciously we know there's a whole lot between x and z. True, it's just one letter. But have you ever been y? Do you know what y feels like, looks like, smells like? Probably not. Even if you've had some y experiences, you likely don't know how to sustain that feeling of the experience. Otherwise, you would.

Micro-steps are so small, yet so powerful. They can take us from a lower vibration to a higher vibration almost instantly. Each step doesn't transform our whole selves, but collectively they contain the power to do so. Here's a personal example to illustrate this point. When I signed the contract for this book, I immediately felt overwhelmed. To finish the book required formulating about 50,000 words, as well as organizing them, and then editing the entire manuscript. That on top of a list of clients and a new house seemed too much. Although I wanted to write the book, I found myself distracted by other things. I became overwhelmed and began to distract myself because to start the book meant I couldn't stop, and I couldn't conceptualize the whole project. My self-talk was something like "I'm not ready. I need to wash the dishes or trim the hair on my dogs' legs."

I was confident that completing the book would be a nine or 10 vibrational feeling, which I welcomed. But I'm working with an eight to 8.5 most days and it was hard to visualize jumping to a 10 from there. That's what causes overwhelm; too great of a distance between where we are and where we want to be. Without a process, we become paralyzed. I applied the AAA Method, and here's what that looked like:

- I acknowledged that I had a book to write.
- I accepted the deadline to fulfill the contract to make this book happen.
- I needed to take some kind of action. A micro-step.

- I asked myself what micro-step I could take.
- I could sit and write one sentence.
- Then, I just did it.

In writing just one sentence, I became engaged in the book, however briefly, and that engagement helped take me into a higher energy frequency. I could visualize my book being written, and finished. With one small micro-step, I shifted my vibration from overwhelm at a seven (I can't) to action taking (I can), which brought me to about a nine. It feels so good. I'm still writing. I can stop now, or I can continue. That is up to how I feel emotionally, physically, and mentally. But I took the micro-step and shifted from can't to can. From one vibrational level to the next.

When you achieve something, no matter how small, you build confidence that shifts you to a higher state. And that movement can take you from not writing a book at all, to being engaged in the book by writing, and eventually finishing the goal. The micro-steps keep you from staying stuck in old patterns. The same principle can be applied to building healthier relationships.

What can you do right now to raise your vibration, however slightly, within the context of your relationships? What micro-step will help you move through fear, and into the present moment with love? Maybe that's being a bit more vulnerable. Maybe it is showing your true emotions or taking a risk and inviting someone to enjoy a nature walk. Don't let overwhelm of correcting the entire relationship stop you from stepping toward your own personal growth. Remember, as you shift your energy, others will feel that. They will be forced to either align to it, or it may open the conversation for much needed change.

A business coach once told me "Leah, you are setting such high expectations, not because you believe in yourself, but because you don't." That was a mind-blower. Of course, I was immediately defensive, because that was my natural response to protect my ego. But once I realized that he wasn't trying to take me down, I was able to internalize what he said. When we put the bar so far out there (seeking to jump directly to a nine from a five vibration—in relationships this is akin to making mental plans for the wedding on the first date), somewhere inside we know this expectation isn't attainable immediately, and maybe not even in the near future. Setting unrealistic expectations distracts us from taking the small steps that build confidence as we achieve success, keeping us connected with our pain.

Setting goals is important. But the lack of a plan or tools to do the work in moving from a five to a nine vibration will leave you feeling frustrated, and keep you stuck in old patterns. When you change your vibration, it changes everything—how you look at the world, and how you relate to people. When you vibrate higher and are able to sustain that, you'll begin to attract people who have a similar energy frequency. If you then encounter someone with a lower vibration similar to your baseline, you may feel the pull toward your "comfort zone" until you consistently apply the tools of the AAA Method.

To raise your vibration in a healthy way, do it slowly, consistently, and consciously. Don't seek the highs or lows—seek self-love instead. Take micro-steps to build confidence in new patterns, and learn to trust yourself by sustaining new patterns in an ongoing way. That's growth. That's achievable.

Chapter 3
Recognize Your "Truth" from Your "Story"

SUCCESSFUL healing requires examining your story, and recognizing the truth of who you are, independent of your story. Conscious thought is important to healing, and is necessary to find acceptance. How does conscious thought differ from being conscious and having thoughts? Conscious thought is viewing the world from a more mature self, instead of a reactionary, programmed mind working on autopilot. It's the practice of mindfulness and bringing awareness and intention to your life.

Awareness allows you to see from a higher perspective and make better choices that will support everything you do. As we become more aware of our imprints, beliefs, and stories, we can make more mindful observations and are able to interpret the actions and behaviors of others as separate from us rather than extensions of us. In other words, mindfulness allows you to step outside of your limited beliefs and realize that other people's behaviors are not about you, but about them.

Conscious thought and mindfulness are heart-based, not brain-based. Your emotional intelligence is different from your mental intelligence. There's a higher intelligence happening when we become mindful, intentional people. The rational mind can understand reason, but it can be difficult for the rational mind to understand emotions of the heart. Acquiring emotional intelligence requires the same diligence and learning as mental intelligence. The difference is that others cannot teach you how to feel. That is mastered by your own experience, and learning how to step into acceptance.

Children lack the ability to make mature mental and emotional responses. Their ability to respond to others is limited, which is why it's so damaging when parents and caregivers treat them with a disregard for their welfare. When children mature into adults, and with the help of conscious thinking, they are better able to separate out their "natural" response from imprints and choose a path that is more aligned with curiosity, discovery, openness, and trust. But it is a learning process.

It's common to fight what we feel. There's a constant inner conflict that is an attempt to get rid of bad feelings in order to feel better. If we're honest, we know when we use our old stories and patterns to stay in our comfort zone—in the vibrational frequency that matches our emotional imprints. Fighting the negative feelings keeps us separated and disconnected from them, but acceptance keeps us connected to ourselves.

When we acknowledge and accept our truths, the hard edges around painful emotions begin to soften. We don't have to hide, deny, or resist. There's no need to explain or defend ourselves. It is what it is, and it's ours. Acceptance is a strong medicine, like a salve to difficult emotions. With this gentle approach, we send a signal to our inner selves that we accept all parts of us. And guess what happens? The difficult feelings start to subside. With no resistance, feelings are free to process and will eventually transform.

Let's use an example of a child who throws a tantrum to get attention. Maybe the child is hungry, angry, sad, or needs affection. The child yells, cries, bangs dishes, or does whatever is necessary to get attention. If the child is ignored, they become even more creative in their efforts. Scolding makes the child feel hurt and they may withdraw to their room, causing a feeling of disconnection from the parent as well as themselves. The parent feels guilty for being harsh or ignoring the child. Now, a push-pull dynamic is at play in which the parent puts out even more energy to reconnect with the child and alleviate their guilt. What has the child learned from this experience? That he must throw a fit and be punished before he gets his needs met. After feeling punished and ignored, maybe Mom or Dad will validate him, but they may also inform him that his needs are too much. This dynamic can easily become an unhealthy approach to loving.

Imagine the same scenario, but in this case the parent acknowledges what the child needs, accepts this need, and gives the child attention. Generally, the tantrum will subside, and the parent stays healthily connected to their child. If this were a common response from the parent, the child would know that tantrums aren't necessary to get attention and may become more patient because they have historically been able to connect and get what they need.

Now, imagine the screaming child as a negative feeling you carry that is asking for your attention, acceptance, to be heard, cared for, and attended to. When you are feeling "off," I recommend a simple and quick meditation practice based on the AAA Method to help you connect to this negative feeling and reach acceptance. The dialogue goes like this:

> "I feel anger. I notice where I feel anger in my body. I breathe into it, and attempt to soften my body around it with acceptance. Then, I speak to the anger. 'Anger, I feel you. I see you. I accept you.'" Usually, within moments, the anger will lessen and you will reach a sense of compassionate acceptance. With acknowledgment and acceptance, the anger doesn't rage stronger, but instead settles as if to say, "Oh, okay. It's okay to be me, now I feel better."

Acceptance is an integral part of building and maintaining relationships with others. It is also a useful tool to help deal with negative feelings or thoughts. For example, if you're fighting with someone but you genuinely understand their point of view, you should acknowledge their truth and accept their position. When you respond in this manner, your "opponent" no longer has a position to argue because their side is now validated and accepted, and the argument can now become a discussion. Whereas if you keep defending your view or talking over the other person, the argument can go on for days. The same is true with emotions.

When emotions are held or repressed for too long, they block the ability to receive or validate incoming emotions. In denial, emotions get stuck. In blaming others, they get stuck. In subconscious repression, they get stuck. In dissociating from traumatic experiences, they get stuck. The result is to default to other negative emotional patterns, which in turn creates an array of toxic feelings.

Resisting negative emotions is like holding them in prison, and the prison is inside. Not wanting to let them loose and do more harm, we store them away like a dangerous animal because we don't trust ourselves to handle such strong feelings. But negative emotions trapped behind prison doors for too long can transform into rage. Unleashed rage can be dangerous and extremely toxic not only to us, but also to people for whom it is not intended. However, if unprocessed shame is trapped inside, we can grow numb, or disinterested in life in general. Holding shame internally may feel like a safer option, but it's just as unhealthy as it may disconnect your true feelings, your loved ones, and a healthy life.

Many of us believe that if we keep negative emotions inside long enough, they will change, or burn out with exhaustion. But often they grow in strength, determination, and energy, finding sneaky ways to slip through the cracks, distort our perceptions, and attack us without warning. Stress, physical aches, lashing out at loved ones, depression, and apathy are common symptoms of repressed negative emotions. These symptoms range in intensity and frequency depending on the severity of the wound or trauma.

Practicing the art of acceptance is the quickest way to diffuse negative behaviors, reactions, and triggers. Acceptance provides space for the negative emotions to live. By trusting our ability to maturely handle emotions as they arise, acceptance recognizes the temporary and mercurial nature of them. Emotions always shift when we make the space for them to do so. The conscious work of the higher mind can help free them, by giving space and caring attention to the emotional need.

Breaking up with blame and choosing acceptance can be extremely difficult but are keys to our emotional well-being. It's common to desire justice to the person who hurt us, and it can feel unfair to carry so much pain for actions that we aren't responsible for, but these are the growing pains. As hard as it is to acknowledge and accept our feelings, it is the only way to evolve and heal, as well as offer others empathy for their hardships.

Identifying Your Story versus Your Truth

Your story is a critical part of your life experience. It is a combination of the events that happened in childhood through your teen years that formed your experience of reality. Your story is not false because it is actually what happened to you from your perspective. If you wrote a movie that involved all of the people in your life, told in your childhood voice, it would be your story. Your story is a summation of the imprint that is attached to your emotional vibrational baseline.

Your truth is the state of self in the reality of now. You'll often hear people say, "And that's my story," when sharing who they are. But even if our story is an important part of our history, it does not need to define our state of being in present time. It's possible that you have been subconsciously acting from the addictive pattern of false or limited beliefs due to your story, without consciously stepping into the truth of who you are and how you feel now.

It's important to understand the concept of false or limited beliefs as they relate to mental health. Living with a false belief doesn't mean that what you experience isn't real or that you do not know truth from lies. It means that at times you are operating from beliefs that were reinforced by others from past situations in your life, even if these beliefs are not true for you now. Look for your internal truth, as that truth will tell you the reality of the moment, versus the story you may be playing out in your mental, emotional, and energetic bodies. Staying present in the moment can be so grounding and healing because it keeps you in the moment of now—not in the memory of then.

Recently, a client of mine who is a mother of three said that she doesn't feel capable of being a mother. Although the reality is that she's in the midst of doing the very thing she feels incapable of doing. She birthed and has deeply cared for each child for many years, which is no easy task, and she has a healthy and happy family to prove it. But her internal dialogue, coming from her inner child who developed insecurities and false beliefs about her limitations, is running her emotional programming. She is living out her story, not her truth.

She perceives her life through the lens of a terrified and pained child instead of her conscious adult self because she didn't get what she needed as a child. She's operating from an emotional deficit that is tied to her emotional imprint. How can an insecure child raise three other children? She feels like she can't, but in reality, she does, even though she's plagued with a sense of insecurity every day. She doesn't feel like she can own her new reality and truth because to do so would abandon her false belief system, and that's all she's ever known. As we worked to reprogram her subconscious by building new thoughts, re-parenting her inner child, and raising her self-love and confidence levels, she has been able to step into her adult self and experience more joy and peace as a mother.

We'll get deeper into inner child work in the next chapter, but I want you to begin to see how all of this ties together. Separating your stories from your truths is important to develop trust in your worth and to build a new foundation. Our stories trap us in false beliefs about who we are, while our truths help lead us to a path of possibility and wholeness. Below are examples of how childhood stories can replay throughout our adult lives.

Example 1

Your mother was addicted to pills. When she was high or about to get high, she may have felt hopeful, lighthearted, fun, or accommodating, and you may have felt like she was happy, loving, and trustworthy. But when she was intoxicated, your mom's personality changed. Even if she didn't become a scary monster, she may have become sad, inattentive, withdrawn, hyper, or no longer interested in listening to you. At this young age, you were not able to understand what substance abuse can do to a mind or body. You were simply having an experience that contradicted the experience you had an hour before with Mom. You may have felt like she became upset, not happy, or extremely happy for no reason. Perhaps she mentally checked out and you didn't feel safe or loved at this time. Sadly, there was confusion.

You made discernments and based beliefs on your mother's shifting emotional and mental states while under the influence, followed by judgments on safety, connection, and love. Many children in this type of experience exhibit fear and panic trying to figure out what they can do to again feel safe, connected, and loved. Children (and adults, if they haven't done their personal healing work) internalize the behavior of others as their fault, questioning what they did wrong, what they should be doing better, if they will be loved again, and ultimately do not feel safe or comfortable in this environment.

It's impossible for a child to manage, process, or understand this kind of environment. But just because a child cannot understand what is happening doesn't mean that they do not have feelings about the situation. Unfortunately, they lack the maturity and skills to process their feelings, so they internalize, becoming fearful and angry because it hurts so bad.

All they can do is try to survive. A child will try to understand who they are in relationship to who their mom is and do what they can to be okay. That sets a particular imprint on their system, and will likely affect most every relationship for years to come. When children are hurt they don't often blame the other, they blame themselves. It's not until children are older when they begin to place blame for the bad things in their lives, but by this time they have already adopted the false beliefs of guilt and shame.

Example 2

Your mother was very present, maybe too present, by doting on and coddling you constantly. Maybe you were spoiled with no boundaries or discipline but you knew that Mom loved you to death. She was always there for you, and she provided anything you needed or wanted.

Perhaps your mom had a relationship with a person or people who did not meet her needs. It's likely she was turning toward you to satisfy some of those needs, staying connected to you out of loneliness or insecurity. You had no space, no discipline, and too much smothering, which vacillated between comforting and suffocating.

With so much parental attention it's likely you came to believe that people in general owed you attention, and you should be loved regardless of your actions or personality. You expected the world to give you what you deserved and you held people in contempt when they said no. Your ability to self-limit food, drugs, and money may be difficult, or you may have trouble staying in relationships with people who are overly attentive as it triggers your feeling of suffocation. Any of these issues could become a part of your adult belief system.

Example 3

Your sibling tortured you out of jealousy or rage due to new family dynamics such as divorce, an additional sibling, or a new marriage. You may have grown up being fearful of close friendships, unable to trust those near you not to harm you. Or perhaps you came to believe that you were inferior and silenced your voice to become a wallflower.

Our stories have the potential to play out in various ways throughout our adult lives if we don't apply conscious thought. We associate our past with sensory experiences such as any thought, feeling, smell, color, or sound. Even something like the touch of a fabric can remind us of the imprint that was developed through our stories with the people and events in our lives. No matter how uncomfortable these feelings may be, the imprint that developed is comforting and eventually draws us back to it. Your story is powerful, carrying with it your imprint and emotional vibrational frequency.

It's common to mimic the stories from our childhood imprints in love relationships, jobs, even with our own children. How many times have you heard people say "I'm turning into my mother," or "My boss treats me like a child." Life stories have a great impact on who we are, but we can apply the AAA Method to step out of our stories and reveal our truth to help us stop self-sabotaging by reliving false beliefs time and again. We don't have to deny or ignore our pasts. In fact, it's healthy to embrace them by using conscious thought to acknowledge and accept our stories, and taking action steps to stop them from dominating our lives.

When I was younger, I would sometimes feel alone. Deep loneliness. Was I alone? No. I had two parents and a sister. I was not abandoned or left wanting. I had family and a lot of friends. I was not alone but I felt alone because of the dynamics with people in my household and close relations. My loneliness mainly stemmed from not feeling understood in my identity as an artist, a lover of spirit, and a sensitive person. I trailed a feeling of loneliness throughout my life, so when I entered into relationships, even friendships, I unconsciously sought people who were distant. In other words, people who were not available. I even sought job opportunities that provided a sense of separation. I was searching for the feeling of aloneness that I had during my youth.

It's not what I wanted. But it's what my emotional and energetic imprints were attracted to because I was using information based on my story and emotional vibration. I found comfort in that feeling.

However uncomfortable I was in the loneliness, there's a comfort in the discomfort. And I was seeking the familiar, safe place of discomfort because that's what I knew. It was my story.

But it doesn't have to be my truth now.

If you recognize patterns in relationships, avoidance, intimacy, trust, shame, unworthiness, or other issues, examine your story to better understand the emotional imprint your story has ingrained in you. Once you acknowledge and accept that you are magnetized back to your story, then you take the action steps to heal.

AAA Method

Acknowledge familiar patterns you are playing out from your story.

Accept that your feelings or behaviors stem from the story of your past.

Act by creating positive experiences to shift your vibration higher and form new emotional energetic imprints. Some examples may be: practicing being present, calling a good friend, or journaling.

The AAA Method will help you attract other people who match your new imprint. This is how to transform the toxic and painful feelings of the past to positive feelings of the present. Processing this work can feel like you've created new DNA—new energetic pathways that support and validate who you truly are in this moment. Conscious thought and confidence-building exercises will help you develop these new energetic pathways.

When you can acknowledge, accept, and take action to shift the pattern of how you have been living out your past wounds based on your story, it's possible to develop new threads of conscious thoughts and choices. That new threading weaves together to reinforce a new story. You will feel safe and happy. You will live a life you desire rather than being tied to old stories and false beliefs. This is when it's possible to attract people of like mind who are not toxic, but supportive. Trust yourself to experience new situations and relationships.

Differentiating your story from your truth allows you to see the false beliefs that were created from other people's behaviors, not your inherent worth. For the purpose of discerning your story from present truth, let's use a simple question to prompt conscious thought. That question is, "Is this really true?"

- Is it true that you are unworthy because your parent or caregiver with addiction issues wasn't present?
- Is it true that you can't make it on your own?
- Is it true that you aren't smart enough to own your own business?
- Is it true that all artists are starving?
- Is it true that if you have a different religious or political view your family will reject you?
- Is it true that you have to live in a certain location?
- Is it true that if you were to take a risk and follow your heart that you would fail or be unsupported?

The truth is, until you raise your vibrational frequency and consciousness, any person or situation you attract will match the frequency of your old story. This is why we must apply the Method before attempting to establish new imprints.

The same process of seeking the truth works for emotional awareness and intelligence. The more present you become, the more you can recognize moments of truth. You may ask yourself, "Do I really feel this way?" "Do I feel the anger or worthlessness in this moment or is that a feeling I am relating to a past relationship or experience?" Does the feeling of being unsafe have to do with this moment or is it a feeling that is attached to trauma in your past? Is your partner purposefully trying to hurt you, or is your fear coming from being hurt by someone you loved in the past, even if it was your partner in the past? Is the shame connected to an old story? If so, what do you actually feel in this moment? If you currently feel shame, can you accept the shame and take action to create a new emotional imprint?

It is possible to take control and feel good again. Releasing the addiction to pain and our stories will expedite the process. Simply asking yourself how you really feel right now as opposed to relying on the addiction of toxic emotions as your guide can jumpstart recovery from our addiction. In the past you may have felt another way, but how do you feel now? Rather than being magnetized back to your story, how can you focus on raising your vibration in this moment?

AAA Method

Acknowledge false or limited beliefs that are attached to your story.

Accept the story that created those false beliefs or emotional pain.

Act by taking a micro-step toward self-love and healing in this moment. Some ideas may be spending time with new people, writing and expressing yourself more, joining a group or club with people who have similar interests, or pampering yourself.

A helpful healing exercise that applies the AAA Method in a broader sense is to figure out what kind of movie your story would make. If your movie is filled with drama, trauma, and dangerous storylines or characters, you may need to meditate or work with a qualified therapist or healing practitioner to gain emotional support. Part of this work is learning to trust your current adult self to create a safe and committed practice that will build confidence and offer a deeper sense of self-love.

Acknowledge

1. Identify the characters in your story. This may include family members, friends, relatives, teachers, babysitters, or other regularly present people who played a role in your developmental years. Try to include those who were present in your life from the ages of two to ten. List these characters in your journal by name. Also include people who were not always present, but played a key role in your thinking and actions. This may be someone you wanted to be close to who didn't seem critical in your story. Develop two storylines: Main Stars and Supporting Roles.

Accept

2. Write at least three pages that detail your "story." Write it as if you are telling a friend about a movie or book. Include important details including any experiences that made you feel either loved and encouraged or scared, slighted, ashamed, embarrassed, or not smart enough. Be as open and vulnerable as possible.

   For example, I experienced sexual energy and encounters with some of my "best friends" at a very young age. It was inappropriate but also made me feel part of a group, desired, and important. I didn't know what sex was at that time. This experience left me with a certain emotional imprint about physical boundaries, worth, and gender roles. I would list these people as Supporting Roles because they were sideline characters that played an important role in my early development but were not always present. I would write from my current perspective of those encounters as well as the mental understanding of what I thought was happening and the struggle it left inside me. The excitement, the fear, the feeling that I was doing something wrong, but also the confusion of it and how I felt loved in that.

Act

>   3. Review your list of toxic emotions from page 22 and write
>   the word(s) that most correspond with your story next
>   to the corresponding event. Use a red or colored pen to
>   highlight the word. Next to my early sexual encounters, I
>   would have written "ASHAMED" and "CONFUSED" as
>   an example.

This process can lead to a better understanding of our toxic emotions, core wounds, emotional imprints, and vibrational frequencies. Seeing how it all connects can free the subconscious mind of false beliefs and invite in new experience. Your story will never be erased, but you don't have to keep pressing rewind if you use the support of the AAA Method. The characters were real. The experiences really happened. And the combination of these events and relationships created your emotional imprints. It can be triggering to retell your story, but remember that you are doing this to acknowledge your history and find acceptance to be able to move forward and rebuild your operating system.

Discovering Your Truth

Many of us continue to bring the stories of our past forward and often act as the person in the original movie, even when many of the characters and environments have changed. It's important to be fully present and learn to discern what we are actually perpetuating from our past versus the truth of what is now. Guilt often gets in the way of living a healthy life of freedom, and guilt or shame is often attached to our worth. Guilt says, "You did something wrong" while shame says, "Something is wrong with you." Think about the story you just wrote. What is the vibration of that story? Consider how much different, or not, your life is now. Consciousness is the act of being present. Acknowledging your past and accepting it is a step toward healing. Transformation is consciously taking action steps to be in this moment.

When people tell their life stories, and then relate them to what is happening today, it's often clear that they are stuck in their emotional imprint. Why? Because they are consumed by what others think, and they are recreating past situations. Their fear of the future is attached to the unknown. If guilt or shame has been a part of their operating system, they can't imagine a life free of those imprints. This is like emotional scar tissue blocking a healthy flow of energy and possibility. The "easier" way to cope is to continue giving most of their energy away to others. If you enjoy writing or journaling, make a new entry using these questions as prompts:

- Which characters are still in your story?
- Who or what are remaining triggers for you?
- What kind of people and experiences do you want to attract to your life now?
- Who is your current support team?
- Who are the new supporting roles or co-stars in your life and what would you write about your life today?
- Which behaviors are you repeating?
- What is your vibrational feeling today? This week? This month? This year?
- How do you spend your time and are you doing what you love?
- What is it that you love about your life, and what do you feel you need to change?
- Have you been successful in maintaining healthy relationships with others? Name those healthy relationships and find gratitude in your heart.
- What hobbies do you love and how do you feel when participating in them?

Practice writing your truth and accepting that truth. Your truth is the foundation for everything else in your life. Write in a way that enhances the qualities you have, even if you don't feel as strong as you'd like in the moment. Remember, you are creating new moments every moment. There will be plenty of chances to practice. Start with the basics to be reminded that you're making progress building new imprints and healthier vibrations. You are doing a good job.

Becoming Present

Tune in to this precise moment and take a breath. Be present right here, right now. Notice the room. How does it feel? Do you experience anxiety right now, in this space? Are you safe here? Learning to step into this moment is the path to recognizing the truth of your current reality. It is scary as we walk one step further from our stories, but it's an important step to rebuilding the life that we desire. Freedom comes when you recognize that in this exact moment, you may actually feel more relief than you believed. The freedom comes from present awareness that you do not have to be trapped by the story of your past if you step into the now.

You may be having an anxiety attack in this moment, and that would be your truth. If you are not having an anxiety attack in this moment, do not claim that you have anxiety, as that only reinforces previous uncomfortable experiences. Reinforce the fact that you do not have anxiety in this moment, and shift your vibration toward feeling good rather than the expectation of feeling bad.

It's important to recognize and accept that much of your story has shaped you, but it doesn't have to dominate or control you. Become empowered with the choice to be present and take micro-steps to maintain control. This does not mean denying, it means acknowledging, accepting, and taking action in the now. As you come to realize that many of the feelings you think you have are not connected to this present moment but to the imprints of your past, the grip on those negative feelings will lessen in intensity, allowing for the current flow of feelings to process.

Chapter 4
Heal Your Inner Child

As we keep moving forward in this book, we'll focus on more specific ways to take action and heal. Inner child work is very helpful in discovering and healing the root of our adult issues. The more progress we make, the more we rebuild the energy matrix of our emotional imprints.

Your inner child is an expression of childhood experiences that are brought forth to the present. Negative childhood memories that remain active in your subconscious mind can trigger physical responses or emotional reactions in adulthood. Your inner child isn't a separate part of you, but also not the entirety of you. Everyone has an inner child, and learning to access it is important to personal growth. As you increase your overall vibration, you will increase the vibe of your inner child as well.

The emotional imprints you developed from childhood memories have an effect on your belief systems and vibrational frequency in adulthood. Not all of the memories are bad, and your inner child isn't a reflection of only negative experiences. Working with the inner child should also bring forward hopes and dreams we can call upon to expand our current reality and joy.

Healing your inner child is an important action step of the AAA Method that allows you to move toward healthier relationships and experiences. Some strategies to work with the inner child are listed in this chapter. Working with your inner child will be an experiential process, and doing the work will reap rewards, including:

- Deepening self-love
- Increasing self-confidence
- Learning to create boundaries
- Accessing repressed feelings
- Connecting with joy through play
- Feeling a full range of emotions
- Finding compassion for self and others

When children are scared, hurt, or do not get what they want or need, they tend to act out their pain or repress their feelings. Children who were abandoned, abused, or suffered other trauma tend to repress their feelings of fear, pain, or shame to avoid further scolding or rejection. As feelings are repressed, our tendency is to avoid relationships or situations that threaten our sense of security—no one wants to feel more hurt.

When the inner child experiences extreme insecurity or trauma rather than emotional support, the reaction may be to mimic childlike responses, making it difficult to achieve healthy, happy adult relationships. Without realizing it, adults often act out the fears and emotions from their inner child's wounds. Part of the healing process is learning when we are reacting to the world from the place of our inner child.

Much of our unprocessed trauma and emotional dysfunction stems from the negative emotional imprints of our inner child. Some experts believe trauma stunts developmental growth at the corresponding age that an event occurred. The AAA Method can be helpful in healing the inner child's wound at any stage and learning to re-parent that part of self to attain a sense of wholeness. First, you will reconnect with your inner child. Next, you will become aware of when your inner child is triggered or acting out in present time as well as attempting to teach you healthier behavior. With practice, it's possible to discern the child from the adult and the past from the present. As you learn to re-parent your inner child, you can move on from negative emotional imprints to rekindle passions and positivity.

Learning Who Is Present

Determining if your emotional reaction or behavior is coming from your inner child or adult self involves staying aware of your original emotional imprint and vibrational baseline. This awareness comes down to the question, "Is my inner child running my life right now, or is my adult self present, using conscious thought and tuning into my emotional body?" Experiencing emotional triggers often comes from unhealed childhood pain, but if you make a conscious effort to remain in the present, you can gain more control over your emotions and ability to respond. When your inner child gets triggered, you may feel any of the following:

- Threatened
- Defensive
- Explosive anger/rage
- Vindictive
- Comparative
- An urge to cry
- Judgmental
- A need to run away
- Attacked
- Numb or checked out

Triggered behavior based on your inner child's response allows for tantrums when you don't get your way, punishing others who disagree with you, or feeling left out. It's possible to listen, speak clearly, understand the other's perspective, and generally respond to the incident in a more stable, neutralized way if a disagreement or upset occurs while you are in your adult state. Life events will always be triggers, and your wounded inner child may say, "Wait! Don't forget about me, I'm hurting!" But as an adult committed to personal growth, you can learn to love yourself into health by applying the AAA Method to heal your inner child.

AAA Method

Acknowledge the presence of your inner child.

Accept the feelings and fears that arise from your inner child.

Act to re-parent your inner child with healthy love, discipline, and nurturing.

Meeting Your Inner Child

It may be emotional to meet and acknowledge your inner child if pain blocks so much of your memory. To get started, try this exercise and see what unfolds. Think back to when you were between three to seven years old. Or, if you had more difficult situations when you were older, like parents divorcing, losing a loved one, sexual repression due to shame, abandonment, or abuse, think of yourself between eight and fifteen. For this exercise, rely on the age that first comes to mind, and try not to judge the outcome. Just stay present and compassionate with yourself.

Close your eyes and remember yourself as a child in full detail. Notice your size, what you were wearing, your haircut, face, and any other detail that you can recall. It's helpful to look at family or school photos. Prompt your visual with specific things like your favorite outfit, hairstyle, or toy. Notice the environment. Are you in your bedroom, the family room, outside, etc.? Where did you often spend time and why? Visualize yourself in your favorite place, or a safe place, where you could often be found. For me, I had a pile of rocks down the street where I would go to "hide" or be alone and feel connected to myself.

Next, imagine yourself as an adult observing your childhood self in this environment. What do you see? Are other people around, and if so, what are they doing? What emotions, body language, or facial expressions are displayed by your childhood self? Allow yourself to go deeper to experience the memories and emotions that arise. Connect with the energy of your inner child as much as possible by observing and tuning in from this perspective.

Now, visualize the possibility of your adult self magically going back in time to this same physical space. Your childhood self, turning and seeing you there, runs and jumps into your arms with amazement and glee. There is an immediate bond that is indescribable. The wholeness satisfies both of you as you connect. You and your childhood self are one, reconnected forever in love, understanding, and compassion. Use your energy and heart to extend as much love as possible to your inner child. In the safety and sanctity of this reunion, notice if your inner child now feels seen, worthy, loved and safe. It's a good idea to record the feelings and thoughts you hear from your inner child. Does your inner child need more attention or a different way to communicate? Ask your inner child and listen without judgment.

Accepting Your Inner Child

By tapping into your inner child's stored emotion and often raw pain and fears, you can better connect with the pure-hearted nature of your childhood self. The more acknowledgment you give your inner child, the greater understanding and acceptance you will have with yourself and others as an adult. Finding acceptance starts with accepting all parts of you, including your inner child.

Let's visualize your childhood self again. Can you accept your inner child for who they are and for their struggles? Even if you don't have full acceptance of your whole self yet, can you feel this for that innocent child? Let your inner child know that regardless of how shy or insecure they may be, no matter how scared or small they may feel, they are worthy of your time, attention, and love.

Tell the child that they are important to the world and that you are proud of them.

We all need affirmation of who we are and what we're about. Remind your inner child of their endearing characteristics. Also acknowledge the sadness, confusion, or pain they experienced, and assure them that you understand how they feel. Tell your inner child that you accept them fully and that they are enough. Hold them tight and reassure them that you have their best interest at heart and that you will help them create a happy life.

Following this dialogue and connection with your inner child, imagine releasing your childhood self while you watch like a loving parent. Your inner child turns and waves, with a new hope in their heart, feeling loved and cared for. As you turn to leave, remember that it's possible to visit your childhood self any time. Return your focus back to your adult self, take a deep breath, and reintegrate into the present moment before moving forward.

Re-Parenting Your Inner Child with Action

After reconnecting with your inner child and internalizing what they need, the next step is to learn how to re-parent your inner child. First we must understand when your childhood self is acting out in order to get their needs met. Because we are so accustomed to old imprints and feelings, identifying our inner child can be confusing, but learning the difference between childhood and adult responses is a major step toward growth.

Recently my inner child was triggered and I was able to move through the situation from a higher vibration by applying the AAA Method. It's another food story (because food is often a relatable issue for many of us). For much of my life I suffered with a sensitive stomach. For most of my teen and young adult years I tried various diets to alleviate discomfort, lose weight, and feel good. Veganism and vegetarianism led to more health issues so I swung to the other end of the spectrum and tried the no-carb paleo diet, finding some relief at various points.

I bought special foods to support my dietary needs but certain family or friends didn't understand my need to eat differently so they poked fun at me, ate my food, and called me overly sensitive. Yes, I was that girl at the restaurant who asked a million dietary questions before ordering. I'm sure the servers wished I had dined at home.

My insecurities and low vibrational imprints at the time led me to feel disrespected and hurt by the lack of support I received from others. Even though I was trying to help myself, I struggled with believing I was worth the effort. My addiction to pain from core wounds was pulling me in and I worried that perhaps the people around me were right. What if there wasn't actually something wrong with my stomach and I was making all of this up in my head? Shame ensued, but after years of enduring pain, a doctor confirmed my gluten intolerance, as well as an intolerance to soy, dairy, and some other foods.

Before being validated, my inner child reactions came forth if other people ate my food. I would get personally triggered because I was left without the food I needed to avoid pain, but mostly because it "made me feel" like those who cared for me didn't love me enough to listen and understand me. My inner child would get terrified because my own needs were not being met.

I'd like to offer an example of a time when I excelled at working through a trigger with my inner child. I offered my homemade gluten-free cookies to my partner because I know he loves sweets. I wanted to share a few, but he ate the entire plate of them, and I didn't stop him. A part of me felt proud that he liked my cookies, but the real reason I didn't stop him was because I didn't have good boundaries in place. Due to my former emotional imprints, my fear was that if I brought this up, I may get ridiculed or called selfish and feel emotionally abandoned. There was a whole container of "regular" cookies in the cupboard. I didn't remind him of that, nor did he seek them out. He was just enjoying what was put in front of him.

The next day after lunch, he ate snacks that he brought, none of which I could enjoy. And I was left with no dessert or snacks because he'd eaten all my cookies. I was so upset and wanted to cry but instead got mad and stormed out of the house. When I got to my car, I caught myself feeling like a child, and recognized that familiar and terrible low vibration.

AAA Method

I **acknowledged** that my inner child was activated and that the fear and insecurities I was experiencing were a result of my old story.

I **accepted** the fear that I was feeling.

I then **acted** to subside that fear by consciously stepping into my higher self and becoming mindful of my present-day self. I soothed my inner child, bought cookies I could eat, and enjoyed those cookies.

I called my partner from the car as I was driving to buy new cookies and told him that I wasn't upset by his behavior, but by an old, unresolved feeling. I replayed a story in my mind and emotional body that he didn't care because his behavior triggered memories of the people who had made negative comments about my diet and sensitivity. Sounds petty, but it pushes my buttons.

The truth is, in that moment with the cookies, I was upset with myself. Yes, my inner child got triggered and I felt invalidated and unloved, but mostly I was upset that I didn't use clear boundaries that I had been working on in the relationship. I knew my partner was eating all of my cookies. While I wanted to be caring and generous, the real truth is that I was acting from an imprint of codependency by offering him my cookies rather than asking for what I needed and telling him where "his" cookies were.

He did nothing wrong. He simply took my offer and enjoyed the cookies. It's not his job to manage my food needs. I should have stepped into my higher self and used healthy boundaries rather than trying to win his affection by over-giving. For example, I could have said "I made some gluten-free cookies and am happy to share one or two, but I'd like to keep them for myself to enjoy. There is a container of other cookies you can eat in the cabinet. May I get them for you?" I know he would have fully understood and not been offended.

But I didn't.

Working on our stuff is a constant process. It feels never-ending, but staying the course is part of the healing journey. Eventually it becomes part of your lifestyle. One of the best places to work through our stuff is in relationships. It helps if the other person has a similar mindset and commitment to healing which offer you a safe place to share. If not, you may endure quite a struggle. The most important thing is to be in the company of others who can either accept you or discuss the process with you so that you can experiment in new ways to break the pattern.

After my mini-tantrum about the cookies, I apologized to my partner for taking my feelings out on him. He understood and was glad I shared my experience, reassuring me that he's there for me. We ended that one in peace, but sometimes it doesn't go so well. For this one example of successfully working through a trigger with my inner child, I have one hundred more examples of failure. It's hard work, but use of the AAA Method makes it much easier. Learning to re-parent your inner child takes commitment, discipline, attention, and love. It's helpful to know that as you create a stronger presence within your adult self, the inner child and the adult have the opportunity to grow together at a more rapid rate.

Discipline comes from a place of love. An undisciplined, unruly, unattended child does not feel safe or loved in the world. When children feel safe to explore more about themselves, they are encouraged to become who they truly are. Offering your inner child new disciplinary guidelines is an opportunity to participate in life expansion by better defining what your adult and childhood selves need.

When our active inner child wounds cause repetitive triggered reactions, discipline should be firm, but being too harsh can encourage more self-sabotage or unhealthy coping skills. Healthy discipline is helping your inner child understand what positive boundaries mean and that setting boundaries does not mean neglecting or ignoring their needs. If you feel like your inner child is acting out in your life, you can overcome the urge to react by giving your inner child healthy boundaries and assurances of how to more healthily emote. As an example, I had to soothe my own inner child. If I used harsh discipline with my inner child, such as "Leah, you're being selfish and too sensitive. Get over it!" I would only affirm the negative feelings from my story. My inner child doesn't need more scolding, harsh energy, abandonment, or correction. She needs to be loved and understood. Here is another example of healthy discipline:

If something in your relationship triggers you but you are unaware of why you are upset, angry, or emotional, take a moment to check in and think about the potential reasons why your inner child may have been activated. Perhaps your inner child is experiencing guilt or a deep sense of shame, remembering times that you felt abandoned and afraid of being left alone. Acknowledge your activated inner child, accept the triggered response as a real emotion or pattern that needs attention, and give yourself compassion, which includes acknowledging the difference between your adult and childhood selves. Reassure your inner child that you hear them and that it will be okay, but right now you need to attend to adult things like working on your relationship. Let your inner child know that this evening you will sit with them and share any feelings, fears, and/or thoughts that need to come forward. Set a time and make a date to be present, feel, and process.

This type of discipline honors the separation of the inner child and adult. As the adult, be clear that you are the one making decisions and creating boundaries. You are in charge, not your inner child, but offer your presence and compassion to your inner child's needs. When you re-parent with love, your inner child will settle down with the knowledge that there is time and space for them because they matter, and will learn how to develop in a safer, healthier way.

AAA Method

Acknowledge the triggered and scared child.

Accept the feelings that are activated.

Act by taking a micro-step forward such as carving out a specified time to process your emotions.

Some recommended action steps in working with your inner child would be:

- Speaking or writing to your inner child
- Playing music and dancing
- Screaming into pillows to free emotion
- Meditative coloring
- Taking yourself and your inner child on a picnic
- Calling a friend

Whatever your inner child needs to feel safe and loved, make time to provide that. Being present and aware of your inner child is a major step toward self-discovery and transformation. Relating to and re-parenting your child in healthy ways will offer assurance that they have support, attention, and love from the person they love and trust the most.

Honoring Your Inner Child

Consider making a physical space in your home to honor and stay connected to your inner child. Perhaps you can create a special altar as a sacred space devoted solely to your inner child. In this special area, add a photo of yourself as a child around the age you visualized in the exercise on page 72. Put the photo in a frame and make it the centerpiece of your altar. Include things you love on the altar as well as something alive such as a plant or a small fountain with moving water and some natural elements such as herbs, shells, crystals, or wooden figurines. You could also place items that your inner child enjoys, or those that recall a fond memory. Think hair clips, arrowheads, or marbles. The altar should reflect a tribute to your childlike energy. You can add any other lovely goodies that have meaning for you, but make sure these items are not associated with other people or experiences that carry guilt, shame, disappointment, or other negative emotions. This is a sacred space to love and honor you.

My altar includes a picture of me in third grade, a plant, crystals, shells, a collection of wooden elephant figurines I've loved since I was a little girl, a Tibetan prayer wheel, and a small piece of floral art from a friend. Sometimes I add fresh flowers or my favorite jewelry pieces I inherited from my grandmother.

This altar should be displayed where you can access and visit it regularly, like in your bedroom or meditation space. As you tend to the natural elements on the altar by watering, pruning, and touching, you can pause and create a deeper sense of compassion and connection with your inner child. These actions help build an ongoing relationship with your inner child, potentially the healthiest parental role you have had.

Alternate Hand Journaling

One of the most productive ways to cut through patterns and communicate with your inner child is to ask questions. When I was struggling with my own healing crisis, I worked with several holistic psychologists and healers. One of them suggested a simple yet effective exercise called alternate hand journaling. It helped me so much that I often suggest it to clients as an ongoing part of their growth.

Dedicate a journal or coloring book as a means of communication with your inner child. Perhaps choose a playful cover. Whenever you are triggered or doing self-care work, write back and forth in this journal or book, talking to your inner child. Here's how this is done:

- With your dominant hand, ask your inner child how they are, or what they need today. Just a single question is fine.

Remember, you are communicating with someone who has limited language skills and emotional capacity. Keep this simple.

- Using your non-dominant hand, write the response from your inner child. This may be frustrating, but that's okay. Writing from your non-dominant hand allows your brain to slow down and hear the inner child. Young children are typically challenged to write and share emotions, so this aligns with their natural state. The response from your inner child may be short or simple as well. Just start a dialogue in this safe place of your journal. Check back when you are feeling a bit off, anxious, or triggered.

Talk with your child and be curious. Your inner child may reveal that they need more downtime, or they may be fearful. Your inner child may let you know that they don't feel safe with your new love interest, or something is not right with a certain friendship. Your inner child may need your attention or want you to be more childlike at certain times. Don't filter the response from your inner child. Let them have their own voice and keep in mind that your inner child has wisdom but also limitations. Don't allow the child to dictate to you as an adult, but to inform you where you are emotionally stuck. You can then use the AAA Method to shift that vibration from feeling bad to feeling good.

A good parent doesn't allow the child to have everything they want. But parents should honor what the child says, listen to how they feel, and be the person who validates them, showing discipline and unconditional love. Healthy parents don't judge, they accept. As adults, parents make the best possible decision with the information they have, and that's how you should re-parent your inner child.

Starting a new relationship with your inner child will be the start of a new relationship with yourself and others. If you witness yourself as a young and beautiful being, feeling compassion and the desire to soothe, you are taking bold action steps toward healing and transformation. Accepting and finding compassion for your inner child is one of the most loving and important things you can do. Your inner child needs you and wants to grow and develop along with you in healthier ways. A child who feels safe and healthy will develop a higher vibrational imprint. As you re-parent your inner child, you are giving your inner self a second chance to rewrite your childhood imprints and develop into a healthier, happier adult.

Chapter 5
Discover Your Authentic Self

YOUR authenticity is your worth. It's your greatest asset, your most prized possession. You may or may not have friends, a decent job, lover, or beautiful home. There's value in each of those things. But your true worth? It is right inside of you. Your authenticity is the character, personality, and spirit that is yours and yours alone. It's your nugget of uniqueness and your contribution to the universe that adds richness and depth, diversity and perspective—the world needs exactly what you have to offer.

Authenticity is the ability to reveal your true self. To feel safe enough to do so, you need to know that someone has your back. Someone you can trust not to judge you, abandon you, or diminish your character. That someone needs to be you. Why is it so hard to reveal our true selves? Why do we hide, become a chameleon, or put on a front for other people? Worst of all, why do most people lie about who they are?

Fear.

It can be scary to put our most valuable resource on the table. We all fear the emotional risk of rejection, scorn, being laughed at, or otherwise dismissed, as these activate our core wounds. These fears can result in people becoming foreigners to themselves, not taking the time to even know who they are, what they believe in, or what they truly desire. Discovering your authenticity requires honesty and learning how to look within. As you do this, you begin to break addictive patterns and the energy held to false beliefs.

The truth is, we lie to ourselves as much as (or more than) we lie to others. We create a version of ourselves for the world to see to protect who we really are. This is the ego at work, reacting from negative emotional imprints. We tell others we feel okay when we do not. We take jobs that fill our wallets but not our hearts. We dress the way the media tells us to, and extend ourselves in ways that are unhealthy. What we tell ourselves becomes our truth, and when we're not speaking our inherent truth, our lies leave little room for growth.

Can you imagine being completely authentic with everyone all of the time? Giving your honest opinion, wearing your favorite clothes, sharing your deepest desires and passions, acting on your dreams, and openly expressing your feelings? Even considering this kind of behavior can spark internal panic. What would others think? You may not feel able to tolerate their judgment. You may worry about losing your job, marriage, or children's love if you display your genuine thoughts, needs, and inclinations. No one wants to be abandoned or shamed or lose the things we believe make us worthy. Our society tells us who to be, but if we always follow its lead, we often abandon ourselves.

Thinking based on fear not only keeps us from being our authentic selves, it empowers others to dictate our lives and determine our worthiness or our value. We often waste too much time trying to fit in, placing more importance on the opinions of others than our own. Think of the energy that could be put toward our dreams and passions if we weren't trying to satisfy other people's expectations.

When you consider living authentically, it may bring on a sense of angst, a combination of fear, anger, and disappointment toward yourself that separates you from your true spirit. There's no need to feel like a rebel for being you. It should feel natural to be you.

Recently I've been working on a 180-year-old house that needs a major overhaul. When I put the computer down, I'm going to turn up the music and dance and sing while I caulk the door trim wearing my painter paints, torn sneakers, and three-day-old hair bun. I might cry if a good song moves me. I can't wait. I am in my glory and feel like a nine-plus vibration. There's nothing to prove, no triggers or emotional addictions, and no one to impress. I get giddy with excitement after completing each minor task and can't wait to share this feeling with others. When I'm in my authenticity I feel safer to relate to the world. If *Vogue* magazine came for a photo shoot to capture the "real" Leah, this is what they'd get.

But if I'm doing a video for social media or on television, I'm likely to pull down my hair, throw on some lip gloss, hide my arm flab with the right shirt, and move the camera to the room with the best lighting. Yes, it's socially acceptable, and I could say I'm doing it out of respect for the viewer, but the hard truth is that I still have insecurities in sharing parts of myself that could be judged as ugly or not good enough. To avoid that rejection, I do what's expected, showing my "acceptable" self and hiding my more vulnerable self. After years of working toward authenticity, I've come a long way, which I'm happy about. More sharing without makeup or filters, and I can't wait to free the rest.

Looking our best makes us feel good, and I enjoy that too. We are all multidimensional beings. But it's important to be aware of when we are not being authentic, of when we are hiding in shame, fear, or guilt. Be alert to when you act out your emotional imprints rather than your authentic truth. Having on the "right" outfit or being socially "acceptable" doesn't equate to a higher vibration. Owning your authenticity increases the vibration of your frequency.

When no one is looking, who are you and what do you enjoy doing? When you feel most at peace with yourself, what kind of outfit, environment, or people are around you? How can you share that with the world? Asking yourself these simple questions can be very challenging to answer. If your mind asks you to judge yourself or it fears being judged by others, you may be experiencing a lower vibration attached to a false belief or wound from your emotional imprints.

AAA Method

Acknowledge that you are judging yourself in fear of how others perceive you.

Accept this feeling of judgment, even though it's uncomfortable.

Act by applying compassion for the insecurities and fears associated with your emotional imprints. Sit with your inner child and grieve the loss of self you've felt throughout your life.

Your True Nature

It is very important to separate our learned behaviors from our true nature. "That's just who I am." "That's just my nature." Sometimes these words come out of our mouths as justification for poor behaviors. Reflect on your true nature. You were not born as an anxious, angry, or defensive person. You did not come into this world with a vibrational frequency of a two or three. While we have innate wisdom to grow and develop our true nature, defensive reactions and learned behaviors are projected when we fear our worth.

The truth is, you were born perfect, and everything else was learned. You may be a quick-witted thinker, but your nature is not sarcastic. Sarcasm is a learned behavior to protect your fear of intimacy, vulnerability, or worth. You may have great empathy for others, but you were not born to fix others. You may have feelings of anger or resentment, but you were not born angry and resentful. Learned behaviors are not who you are. You are behaving in those ways because you did not learn how to safely process your anger, fear, or feelings of insecurities and still receive love.

Children absorb energy and emotions as information. If your lineage included ancestral trauma or you experienced emotional wounds or medical emergencies while in the womb, you may have absorbed negative patterns or beliefs from your mother. While some could argue that children are born with less than a ten vibration, those conditions were still learned. We were all born with a ten vibration, innocent and pure beings full of love and wonder. Over time, we developed negative and fearful responses that lowered our vibrational frequency. We learned to talk quickly in order to protect our vulnerabilities. We learned to interject with volume in order to be heard. We learned to fear emotional situations that terrify us, or that we've seen harm others. The responses we form are either survival mechanisms against real danger or emotional defenses to protect us from perceived danger and to feel safer in the world.

It's possible to reprogram your patterns with higher awareness. The next time you are in a difficult relationship pattern and want to defend yourself, use the AAA Method. If, for example, your go-to response to perceived danger is to use sarcasm, practice the following:

AAA Method

Acknowledge that sarcasm has previously helped you cope with negative self-beliefs.

Accept that you feel unworthy of being heard, loved, or validated and that you use sarcasm to defend this fear.

Act by taking deep breaths or journaling your feelings, and remind yourself of your true nature as you attempt to respond differently.

When you are triggered, upset, or feel defensive, try this shortcut to return to your true nature: "This is not who I am. This is a reaction to difficult past experiences, and I have a choice to respond differently." Bring your focus inward, soothing your inner child if needed, and remember who you are.

Interacting with others from a place of authenticity can make us feel very vulnerable. Remember that your vulnerability likely comes from the fear of not being enough, not from your true worth as a divine being. As you practice the AAA Method and build up your authentic sense of self, you will gain confidence and attract those who are vibrating at a purer and higher frequency. Living authentically, you will never be alone.

This work is the call of the higher self. The allure to heal and have a happier life comes from a deep inner knowing that you are much more than the experiences you've had. The higher self craves to vibrate at a higher frequency, to feel light and free. It is asking the conscious mind to remember, and to find the way home.

Here's a personal story about inauthenticity. For many years I worked in the media, owning a small production company and working as a freelance TV host and on-air talent. As a young girl I had a dream of working in television and somehow making a difference in people's lives. It was a dream come true when I moved to Los Angeles and then NYC to attain my goal booking jobs along the way. While I loved the media industry, as I grew older, I realized that part of my dream was the need to be validated because I didn't feel good enough as much as the love for media itself.

One year I decided to pursue my interests and apply as a producer in the large market of NYC. I wasn't necessarily qualified for the big league, but I was determined to somehow prove my on-air hosting chops, and I used this back-door approach to reach that goal. I sent my resume to *Good Morning America*, CNN, and other major television production companies. I had a few mutual contacts from having already spent years in the industry, but most of my job search was made up of cold calls and email submissions online. It was a complete shot in the dark. I heard nothing from my submissions. Not even a chirp. Months and months of silence.

About a year and a half later I was camping in the woods with a friend and enjoying the great outdoors, hiking with my dog, and eating bad food over a fire, when out of the blue I received a call. From CNBC. They informed me that they had kept my resume on file and were calling to request an interview for a web producer position on *Mad Money with Jim Cramer*. I was beyond excited! In that moment I visualized this high-powered title, lots of money, possible fame, and a chance to meet the who's who at CNBC and impress them with my talent. The sky was the limit. Perhaps hosting an on-air national TV show wasn't that far-fetched after all.

I spent at least a week shopping for the "right" skirt. (Of course, what I had wasn't good enough.) I found the right one—just to the knee, black, not too tight, but fitted—that I believed said, "I've got my act together." I paired my outfit with super high heels I'd only worn once to a wedding. I'm not sure what I was thinking, except maybe that I was trying to get tall enough to be noticed. They were not quite spike, but almost, and I was severely uncomfortable in them. Looking back, I've made other poor wardrobe choices, all out of insecurity and trying to look a certain way, but this one was the worst. I couldn't walk in those shoes. Not even for five minutes, much less the hour-long tour they had planned to take me on around the studio. They were interviewing me to be a producer, not a fashion model.

The interview came. Everyone else was in casual attire, as these people worked twelve- to sixteen-hour days. They had no time for heels. Overall, the interview went well, but the entire time I was thinking, *This isn't me. This isn't what I want. I have no interest in getting sucked into a big corporation, no matter the title or accolades. I don't want to become a producer on a financial show.* I really didn't know why I was there besides trying to show myself and the world that I was good enough to be validated by a big media company. My ego was fed, that was about all. I wobbled out of CNBC with blisters on my heels, numb toes, and a good dose of humility.

The follow-up call was friendly as they informed me that although I was one of the finalists, they chose a more experienced producer who was able to work nights and had more experience. I imagine my shoes screamed, "I don't do the graveyard shift!" Sometimes I wonder where life would have taken me if I had been offered that job. And for that reason, I'm glad I wore the heels.

If I were being authentic, I would have realized that I didn't want to produce that show and graciously declined the interview. But I didn't. Was it a waste of time? Not in my book. That experience helped lead me closer to my authentic self in a way that I wasn't capable of on my own. It bruised my ego, but opened my heart.

Had I taken the job, I would have wrestled with my authenticity for years. A good income with great benefits is important and alluring. But is that enough? Not for me. Maybe it's not for you, either. I can laugh now, but I wonder what the woman who gave me the tour must have been thinking.

It's common to make all kinds of justifications, rationales, excuses, and reasons for why we say or do the things we do. What if an opportunity comes along for a relationship with someone who looks the part, and seems to be a good fit, but you don't feel comfortable revealing your true self? Maybe the person doesn't understand your history. Maybe they don't have an interest in spiritual growth. Maybe there are red flags that attract your former emotional imprint of a four vibration but you're aiming to sustain the frequency of an eight? Yet you pursue the relationship anyway.

When making choices, ask yourself if you are consciously choosing from your authentic and empowered self or your lower vibrational imprint. You may be better suited with someone who doesn't meet your preconceived idea of "the right one," but rather a person who matches your new and higher frequency that may, at first sight, not feel familiar. Perhaps you prefer someone who is living intentionally, who may not be the wealthiest or prettiest, but has a tender heart, and encourages you on your path. You may choose the person your parents or friends may not understand, because they still view you from a lower vibrational frequency as part of your family imprint. It's important to do your own personal work to acknowledge and accept your previous patterns and act to heal the hurt. Only then can you discover your most authentic self.

As truth tellers, the opportunity to live a peaceful and authentic life becomes reality. Speaking our truth may cause the loss of a few friends, and while painful, the truth will set you free to attract people with whom you can resonate your highest vibration. Self-exploration is the means to look at both the pain and the beauty that make us who we are. As we become more and more honest with ourselves, we may notice when we react to the world and others from a place of defensiveness instead of authentic strength. These behaviors reinforce the negative or toxic emotions we hold on to for safety, keeping us disconnected and distant from true peace, love, and happiness. Shifting to love is courageous.

Loving the self is powerful. It's learning to soothe, not scold. It's learning compassion, not self-sabotage. It's learning to apply the energy and care we give so freely to others, to ourselves. Love is the most healing therapy in the world, yet it is hard to access if we haven't worked through our limited false beliefs and core wounds. When you're honest with yourself, it's possible to respond to red flags immediately. There's no need to convince yourself of anything when you're living in your authenticity. There's no need to fix others. You will either accept people as they are if you feel strong enough not to be pulled to a lower vibrational pattern. Always trust your feelings, and if something doesn't match what you need, move toward what does.

Identify your internal language to maintain an honest and authentic perspective of your foundation. It takes presence and acceptance to eradicate long-held, difficult emotions such as these:

- "I'm trying to find myself."
- "I don't know who I am."
- "I am identified by the labels of others."
- "I am not special."

- "My family operates like this, so I have to operate like this."
- "I've never pursued the life that I wanted."
- "This isn't what I expected."
- "That's just my nature."
- "My life looks unrecognizable."

Our identity is often based on a conceived idea of worthiness relative to a specific function, person, or job. Value is a subjective thing. The power of the mind is so strong that it can create an entire belief system around the perspectives, thoughts, or emotions of other people. As adults it's important to think about what we actually believe as truth about ourselves, and surround ourselves with healthy people who support us in breaking old patterns that diminish our worth.

There's a distinct difference between how you view yourself and how others view you. We often judge ourselves against what other people think of us or believe us to be, but our judgment is subject to old inner wounds and emotional patterns. If we try to live another person's version of who they think we are, or want us to be, we will forever feel lost and unanchored in our authenticity. Personal authenticity and acceptance is the security you need to blossom into your most divine self. Discovering and claiming the truth of your authentic self will allow you to direct love and healing to the places that need it most.

Given that our values come from the people we respected, loved, and depended upon as children, any hints of disapproval from these people could have instilled a false belief that something is wrong with us.

Our present-day value can also be determined by interactions with people we don't know well or at all. We judge ourselves against friends with more or less money, celebrity lifestyles, or other people's relationships. We try to make sense of our value in relation to most anything, and when we don't understand or trust something, we're often left with insecure feelings of what or who we should be.

Who You Are

The below exercise is an important first step to discover who you really are. Include a thorough intake or inventory of yourself, including negative beliefs and perhaps grandiose beliefs. Throw it all onto the page and purge every single one. An unfiltered look at yourself may feel scary, but hiding from it will trap the negative energies. Be completely honest, unfiltered, vulnerable, and willing to own all parts of yourself. This allows you to better understand the false beliefs of your "stories" and begin to clear toxic energy so you can vibrate higher in your truth.

In your journal, reflect on this question: "Who am I?" Describe who you are without any filter or judgment, and refrain from identifying yourself in relation to another person. Do not identify yourself as a mother, father, friend, wife, or employee. Instead, use great detail to describe yourself and the inherent qualities that make you who you are. Be specific and as vulnerable as possible. Write whatever comes to mind.

For example, I am a tenderhearted, sensitive woman. I'm a strong presence in my community, yet I feel extremely vulnerable in personal relationships. I'm in my middle-aged years, becoming more aware of the value of time, my worth, and aging. Although I'm confident in many areas of my life, I have self-image insecurities. I am gifted with beautiful hair, but as it is beginning to change, I find myself feeling identified with my age and talking negatively to myself. My regrets make me feel vulnerable, but I am very strong in my pursuits of purpose and healing. I love to help others. Sometimes I get angry and feel like a fraud. I'm afraid of certain relationships. I am an artist who loves to paint abstract nature with acrylic paints but most of my art never ends up being the image I first sit to create. I always get frustrated while painting but in the frustration flows creativity that comes out organically, and I just go with that. I am a pianist. I'm a good person but I feel poorly that I don't call my friends as much as I think they would like. In my art I find freedom to be fully me and I feel alive. I am emotional, and sometimes I worry that

I'm too emotional. I feel like people don't understand how I process the world. I express myself with words, laughter, tears, art, music, dancing, and creativity. I'm generally a positive person, but I need a lot of sleep or I get cranky. When I'm alone I feel peaceful, but I'm no stranger to loneliness. I love to enjoy a nice long bath to think about the day and just unwind.

See if you can write at least one page about yourself, two if possible. This is a challenging exercise, but as a living creature, you have many aspects of you to share. When resistance sets in, remind yourself that you are committed to love.

Speaking to Self and Others

How we speak to ourselves confirms our reality. Our internal critical voice is attached to pain. The pain comes out as negative self-talk, a sharp tongue to others, impatience, self-sabotage, criticism, and general discontent. Speaking to yourself with acknowledgment and acceptance is attached to love and honor. Self-trust and self-confidence increase when you speak your truth.

Many of us are masterful at hiding our feelings. We hide behind the clouds of guilt, not wanting to hurt another's feelings, not wanting to rock the boat, or masking our true emotions or needs based on what we think others expect just to make life "easier." We also hide behind clouds of shame such as not feeling smart enough, worthy enough, visible, or important enough to share our ideas and feelings with others. Often we remain silent rather than risk rejection or unworthiness. But learning how to speak out and be authentic is critical to self-love and healing. In fact, I have a saying that "revealing is healing." It's important to practice finding your voice, sharing your authenticity, and claiming your worth with integrity, compassion, and strength to gain new ground in your new life.

Speaking your truth is not to be argumentative, combative, defensive, or insensitive to others. At times your truth may ruffle feathers or create defensiveness in others, but those are their feelings to work through, not yours. Speaking your truth is to be honest, compassionate, and forthright in your expression while still considering your audience. Not everyone will understand you, nor should they. Not everyone will agree or accept what you say, and they don't have to. Trust in yourself enough to accept another's disapproval. If you become triggered from perceived rejection, pause and step into your higher self and apply the AAA Method. When you realize their opinion is not a personal reflection of you, you can then manage your emotions without trying to manage theirs. You can still stand proud in your truth without everyone's reactions causing you to default back to your "story." In time, and with enough practice, these efforts will be beneficial, but the first step is to become confident and speak from your heart.

Confidence can be gained by taking persistent micro-steps toward authenticity. Continue to be honest with yourself to continue your healing journey. The more you engage with integrity in your own life, the more your inner self feels worthy of time, attention, and love. Make sure your heart is open. Meaning, if you are speaking from defensiveness, resentment, and fear, or are operating in protection-mode, it is likely that you are not in touch with your deepest truth. To be fully authentic means to risk being vulnerable enough to say what you need and how you feel. It's scary. But it is necessary.

Speak from your heart even in large groups or presentations. Notice if you are monitoring your words for fear of being judged. Consider your audience, but don't try to become your audience. Authenticity requires you to express your style, personality, emotions, and unique thoughts. You don't have to monitor everything you say if you are being authentic. Authenticity and mindfulness work well together, but trying to be something you are not, or performing instead of sharing (unless you're a performer), will not transmit your authenticity to your audience. Most people, even in one-on-one relationships, prefer to know and see who you really are, not to judge you, but to witness and experience what you have to offer. It makes them feel safer and able to share their own authenticity as well.

It is freeing to be truly authentic. This feeling of freedom may initiate fear, but keep in mind that you are becoming more whole.

Being responsible to yourself doesn't mean you aren't responsible to other people. In fact, the more you show up for yourself in a healthy way, the more you can show up for others.

Determine Your Wants

Create a two-column list. On the left side write "shoulds" and on the right side write "wants." Put a line down the middle and write a list under the "shoulds" column such as "I should eat better." "I should call my cousin more." "I should put money aside for ____." Below your list of shoulds, add statements such as, "If I had done ____ better, or at all." Think about what you're writing. If you had done what, what could have been different? Question if this is or was your obligation or duty as a human being. Next to each should, write the vibrational frequency you associate with it from our scale on page 35.

Under the "wants" column, write another list of the things that you want to do. Some of them may be repeats from the "should" column. "I want to eat better." "I want to go to Paris." "I want a new job." Below your list of wants, add statements such as, "If I ____," and add some possible action steps of how to turn your wants into possibilities and reality. Note next to each want the vibrational feeling you have in dreaming about it or feeling a sense of accomplishment.

Which list is longer or fuller? Does the should list feel heavy, or like too much obligation? Does the want list make you excited and eager? Reframing your internal dialogue and acknowledging what your soul needs is an important step to actualizing a new reality.

Of course, we don't always get everything we want. It's also important to recognize that our obligations can also connect us to feelings of love. An imbalance is only created when you live out the expectations of others more than the desires of your heart. It's your decision to determine how you want to live. The more you identify and question your truth, the closer you will be to your authentic self and a happier life. Empowerment is a major step toward healthier relationships with yourself and others.

Chapter 6

Welcome Self-Love as Medicine That Heals

SELF-LOVE. It sounds so cliché these days. In the commercial market and social media world, self-love and self-care have become the trend, forcing every conceivable form of pleasure or escape in order to live your best life, get your act together, and eliminate pain.

But there is real value in self-love. In healing, it is a step toward empowerment and confidence, and it leads you to the highest vibration possible. There is great reward in allowing the time and energy to love yourself, and it doesn't encourage you to become narcissistic. There's nothing selfish or vain about genuine self-love.

Loving yourself does not take away or diminish the love you have for others. Never. This belief is part of the problem. The idea that to love and care for yourself is selfish comes from an energy belief based in "lack" thinking, which is attached to shame. People who believe that self-love is selfish or narcissistic have limited beliefs about worthiness and abundance and fear capacities to love out of fear they aren't "enough." It's not entirely their fault. Over time they've learned that being a good person means you should put others above yourself. These learned beliefs developed from a place of fear.

It's polite to open a door for someone if you feel inclined to do it. Being polite, considerate, caring, and loving are all wonderful attributes when these things come from the heart. However, if our actions come from a sense of guilt or shame, we cross the line into unhealthy patterns. Impressing someone, fulfilling expectations of others, or seeking approval of others are all examples of unhealthy behavior to prove our worthiness. These are self-serving actions that stem from our emotional imprints.

Self-love does not take away from loving others. It doesn't mean that you are unable to love others because you're too busy loving yourself. Think about it this way. If you love sweet potato fries, and also love chocolate cake, does your love of cake steal from your love of fries? If you love your cousin Suzy and also love your cousin George, do you have to choose which one you love more? Does your love for Suzy make your love for George unhealthy? Can you love the color orange and also love dogs? The point is that it's possible to love yourself fully and still have plenty of love for others. In fact, you will have more.

Some people may try to shame you for loving yourself and not always putting others first. The real shame likely belongs to those doing the shaming. These people typically have toxic shame or guilt, which they try to transfer onto others to alleviate their own suffering. When we absorb that shame or guilt (especially as children), it creates a false belief system that we are not as valuable as others.

This is not true.

Self-love is not only thinking about ourselves, it is also about taking care of our needs in order to establish good boundaries and healthy interactions with others. Subconscious self-blame has its roots in the desire to fix someone else's problem. When we stop putting the problems of others ahead of our own and use conscious thought, we can acknowledge the parts of us that are suffering while participating in relationships with others.

It's your personal responsibility to be healthier, happier, and to experience emotional freedom. It may seem unfair, but you evolve by owning what is yours in order to embody the lesson that was intended for you to learn. Thank those who taught you life lessons. Parents, siblings, mentors, friends, and lovers are your ultimate teachers. Show gratitude for them as you heal and transcend.

Self-abandonment is a subconscious way to keep our wounds safe and to deny our needs. By blaming or attempting to control others, we abandon ourselves. We play small from a limited belief system, put others ahead of ourselves, and let the inner critic or voice of another stop us from chasing our dreams. We stay quiet and do not speak our truth. Ultimately, self-love is learning how to stop this process of self-abandonment.

It's common to abandon our opinions, needs, and dreams. There are always excuses for why we abandon these things, but the truth is that we abandon them because of our fear of rejection and low self-worth. It's difficult to believe that we are "good enough" so we place others in front of us.

Putting Action in the Method

To make the AAA Method effective, we must focus on taking action. Action steps can help support a higher vibrational frequency that leads to happier and healthier relationships, but if we do not acknowledge our story and our truth, and accept where we are now, any action we take will feel like one step forward and two steps back. "Doing" keeps us busy and sometimes distracted, while "being" helps us stay in the moment, learning to be present to our higher self. Consciously being can actually be a very healthy action step. It may be as subtle as shifting your mindset from reactive to conscious thought.

There are many ways to support your personal growth. As a general rule, start with the densest energies first (your physical body) to create a foundation for you to grow. Like a pyramid, start with your self-care and build a strong and sturdy base from which to build. The more grounded you are, the higher you can rise. Physically taking care of your body can help shift emotions, elevate your mood, clear your mind, and raise the vibration of your energy field. Eating well does wonders to create harmony with each of these areas.

As you tend to your physical self, it's a tangible reminder to self how deeply you care. The steadier you feel, physically and emotionally, the more strength you have to raise your overall vibration by addressing the root of your issues. Face your fears and rise up to the challenge of growing. Reassure your inner child that you matter and that you are committed to feeling better.

There's an interesting similarity among people who have low self-worth. They struggle to take action. Without connection to one's worth, it's difficult to make decisions, to risk failing, or find the energy to plan. Self-esteem and action are related. In terms of energy, both self-esteem and action are governed by the solar plexus chakra. Low self-worth causes people to withdraw, wait, and watch. They wait to be chosen, instead of doing the choosing. This is especially true in relationships.

Choosing versus Being Chosen

Waiting to be chosen occurs when you wait for approval and validation from others that you are enough. You are placing your worth in someone else's hands while you sit on the sidelines of your life, hoping for confirmation. Waiting for people to call, waiting for your talents to be noticed, waiting to be asked. Think of all the time we have wasted as we wait to be chosen in many areas of our lives.

A Chooser steps forward from an empowered place as a present and confident person. A Chooser asks for what they need or what they desire. A person who chooses calls the shots, puts their hat in the ring, steps up to the plate, and prepares for their future. They take the greatest action step of all time by choosing their life.

The act of waiting has a lower vibration than proactively choosing. At times you must wait for a response, but that's different than living by default while waiting to be chosen. Think about the second hand on a clock. Imagine it represents the micro-movements of your life. Being engaged in proactive and conscious decisions (i.e. being the chooser), you are constantly in motion toward a healthy and meaningful life. When you wait to be chosen, the second hand is stalled, suspended in time, and only moves forward when someone else decides your fate. This places your power in the hands of others, weakening your position and creating stagnation in your energy, mind, and life.

Choosers have self-confidence and allow feedback from others. They have trust in themselves to grow from any outcome. You might think, *but I don't have confidence*. Be mindful of that negative thinking because false beliefs are attached to your original emotional imprint. You can gain self-confidence each and every day by practicing the AAA Method. If you still feel hesitant about trusting yourself after this exercise, go back and rework the Method around authenticity.

AAA Method

Acknowledge that you have low self-confidence.

Compassionately **accept** that your confidence is low.

Act by taking a micro-step to better connect with your truth such as doing something that you know you're good at, or taking a moment to focus on being here now and reapplying the practice toward something else you may need to improve on.

Becoming a Chooser doesn't mean everyone is going to choose you back. That's okay. The more you step forward with authenticity and express your desires and needs with integrity, the more you will grow into your whole self with more confidence. Choosing allows you to move forward on your terms, taking in each lesson and experience as opportunities to grow.

Years ago when I auditioned in LA and NYC for jobs, I was constantly feeling rejected. The number of times I didn't get callbacks was vastly greater than the times I did get a call. I didn't feel good enough, even though I knew I was competing in large markets, and not being selected was inevitable.

A friend in the industry once said to me, "You can make it in this town if you have the stomach for rejection." At the time, I wasn't sure I had that kind of stomach, but her words helped to shift my perspective. Rejection triggered my lower vibration of false beliefs from old emotional imprints, and I was using it to keep me stuck. I was trying to "win" the approval of casting directors. I was waiting to be chosen.

When I began to go to the auditions as an opportunity to practice and learn, my attitude changed. I could never lose. I began to place less focus on the outcome, and more on the opportunity to hone my skills, meet people in the business, strengthen my vulnerabilities, and share my unique personality. From that point forward, every audition was fulfilling, and I booked a lot more jobs as well!

Being a Chooser is a form of self-love. It is consciously embodying your true self while participating in the world. Being a chooser shifts your vibration quickly from "I'm not sure about myself so I'll let others decide" to "This is something I want to do for myself, and I'll feel great about the attempt, no matter the outcome."

Learning to empower yourself is daily self-care. You don't have to prove yourself, but just be confident in who you are and what you want. When you know that your needs matter, you will no longer wait for approval. This is the way out of self-abandonment.

Meeting Emotional Needs

A very wise therapist once told me, "You are not in relationships to get your emotional needs met. You are in relationships to get relational needs met."

Insert head-blown emoji here.

Children need their parents for support, love, and to teach them how to process emotional needs. As adults we should be able to meet our own individual emotional needs, but many of us expect our emotional needs to be met by our partners. It's not your partner's role to make you happier or to help you process emotional trauma. It's not their job to help you follow your dreams or to make you feel confident. It's not their job to make you feel loved or worthy.

This truth is both liberating and terrifying. My inner child wants to kick and scream, "NOOO!" But it is this truth that helped me to end my chase of seeking validation and unconditional love from "unavailable" people. It places responsibility on where it is meant to be, and breaks my negative emotional imprint. I now know that is not the job of anyone but me. All of us are responsible to meet our own emotional needs. Relationships are started with people as they are, wounds and all. But too often there is an expectation that the person you are in a relationship with is going to heal your wounds, save you, fix you, or make you happy. And vice versa.

We validate ourselves. We love ourselves. When we find our own worth and joy, purpose and satisfaction, we can then enter relationships clearly, being able to experience life with others. Healthy relationships allow us to relate to others and experience life's ups and downs together, sharing support and presence. The healthy and right partner will reflect back to you some of your deepest wounds and fears and will hold the space for you to do your own work while they care about you in the process.

Human contact and connection to others is essential to be healthy. When we are emotionally healthy, we may have a desire for things, but not a needy expectation. Need versus desire is an interesting topic. What are other "needs" that should be expected from others? What do you need that you cannot give yourself as an adult? What do you want from another person? What deficits do you bring to the relationship with the expectation that another person will fulfill? I may want someone to alleviate a burden in my life, but the bigger issue is why am I not handling the situation in a healthier way so that it is not a burden in the first place?

Everyone needs healthy relationships and connection to others, but we should not be dependent on others to make us happy. When stressed, it's common to want empathy and someone to listen to you or hold you. Your emotional needs can be met by seeking therapy, online courses, or support groups with people who can guide and provide support. Relationships are where relational needs are met—enjoying sunsets, watching movies, talking about philosophy, politics, or spirituality. Relationships are created by sharing common interests. You may try new food recipes, enjoy intimacy and laughter, and share music or other interests. You may also relate to one's past experiences or family dynamics, offering compassion and understanding.

It's good to talk to your partner about how you feel and ask for their compassion and wisdom, but it's not healthy to expect your partner to fix you. To address emotional needs, we must learn how to self-soothe, process emotions, shift our energies, and empower ourselves. Social slang calls this "adulting." You may not feel like "adulting" every day. It's difficult. There are times when our inner child cries out, "I need a break! I need to color, play, and rest!" Making time for those feelings is taking care of your emotional health and asking yourself what needs you have and how you can best satisfy them.

Your Language of Self-Love

We each have a language for how we express love to ourselves. I created a simple classification of the language of self-love as follows:

Denier: Little to no acceptance or practice of self-love, denying yourself of loving feelings.

Dater: Superficial pampering, caught in the curious stage but never turning into a deep relationship (just enough to feel good but not enough to fully commit).

Doter: Daily routines of self-love that reflect acceptance, discipline, encouragement, and giving yourself the love that you need.

Learning to love yourself can be an uncomfortable experience if you believe that attention to your wellness is selfish. But like any relationship, we need to practice growing by acknowledging our weaknesses, fears, and trepidations as they arise. The relationship with the self takes great commitment because your accountability partner is you.

Consider the language you use as well as your internal voice when working on self-love. Do you deny, date, or dote in your practice of self-love? Use the following prompts to guide your thinking.

1. I easily take meaningful private time. (Taking time to journal, listen to music, going out to a restaurant, dinner for one.)
2. I care for myself physically. (Practicing good nutrition, seeing a physician if ill, regular maintenance, massage, exercise.)
3. My mental health is a priority. (Prioritizing meditation, slow walks in the park, using new brain muscles, or personal therapy.)
4. I process and attend to my emotional needs. (Seeking counsel, support groups, allowing time to emote, journaling, expressing how I feel, reaching out to others, committing to self-growth, happiness, and wholeness.)
5. I am devoted to my spiritual life. (Active in prayer, meditation, moments of silent reflection, communing with nature, sacred music or rituals.)

If you made excuses or felt guilt or resistance to the above statements, you may lean toward the self-love language of a denier. Denial means using excuses such as "I don't have enough time" or "I'm too shy to spend an evening out alone." If you responded with yes and no answers and a tinge of guilt that you are not doing all of the above statements, you are likely a dater in the language of self-love, meaning you are not sure if you are fond enough to invest. If you enjoyed answering yes to most of the above, you are likely in a healthy, committed (and doting!) relationship with yourself.

Self-love is an art. There is no right way to acquire self-love, but when you use the AAA Method, no other feeling will provide such wholeness. You know the feeling you have when you are unconditionally caring for someone or something from a pure place in your heart? The place that doesn't judge, condemn, or criticize? That is the place where the source of self-love stems. The good news is there is no shortage of love. It may be hard to access at times, especially when we are programmed to hold shame and guilt, but it is always available to those who do the work.

As with many things in life, small but consistent efforts of self-love make the biggest impact. Love doesn't equate to big-ticket experiences. We don't need a weekly massage or trips to holistic spas to fully care for ourselves. We can feel better with small acts of self-love that build esteem, trust, and happiness. This is an inside job that no spa can offer.

Recently I was able to use the Method to deepen my self-love. When my boyfriend stays with me, I get that Sunday morning feeling. You know the feeling of taking it slow and easy, treating yourself to brunch and inspiring music? I like to make us pancakes, turkey bacon, and fruit smoothies on those days. One time I realized that I only make pancakes on those days when he or family members visited. I love pancakes so much, but I only cooked them for special breakfasts with others. Making pancakes for myself felt like a lot of effort, so I didn't bother.

AAA Method

I **acknowledged** my limited thinking and self-denial.

I **accepted** the sadness that I placed more worth on the joy of others than myself.

I **acted** by making pancakes for myself, which has now become one of my favorite meals most every day.

Pancake making is a perfect micro-step toward self-love that took little effort. Enjoying them alone is now a treat, and this act elevates my vibrational frequency every morning. Developing any skill takes commitment, repetition, compassion, and ongoing practice. But you have to take that first micro-step.

Self-love helps comfort and soothe your inner child, and also builds confidence in your adult self that you are worth the investment. These can be small investments or larger ones, but they should all be lovingly positive, reassuring, and achievable. Reflect on how love is expressed to others. Sometimes we give gifts, and other times we may express love by just listening. Or we may send a note to commemorate a special date, or share a song that reminds us of the person. Other times we may feel gratitude and whisper the simple words, "I love you."

When was the last time you whispered those words to yourself?

What a shame that we've been taught that to love ourselves is wrong and selfish. How is it possible that we've been asked to be such loving and giving people to everyone but ourselves? The world could be different if we loved ourselves and did what's best for our hearts. It's time to stop living for the approval of others and focus on what feels right to us.

Silencing Your Inner Critic

Your inner critic is the voice of judgment that says you "should." Sometimes this critic is the memory of a parent's voice, or it may be criticism from siblings or friends. When you hear the voice of judgment, acknowledge it and take stock of your life and your experiences in it as the mind would have you do. But know that you are more than your mind, and the judge you hear does not always have to overpower your compassionate heart and higher self to create inner conflict.

It's easy to hold unreasonable expectations when we judge and compare ourselves to others. Depending on our level of shame or guilt from childhood imprints, we begin to operate based in fear of judgment linked to our worthiness. We use judgment to prove our worth or lack thereof. It is not a healthy behavioral system. Many of us have been taught to ignore, override, or deny the negative thoughts and messages we feel, but the more we acknowledge and accept these messages, the more power we have to change their vibration.

The healthy way to quiet the inner critic is to acknowledge and accept it, then apply new voices and perspectives to act as change agents. These new voices and perspectives become healing balms for the broken spirit.

"I don't know why . . ." or "I've always been . . ." or "It's just the way I am . . . " are examples of false truths that are wrapped around old stories, the false belief systems that were created in our developmental years during stressful or traumatic times. To rewrite these false belief systems and find new truths, we must face our reality and empower ourselves with curious minds, new words, and self-love patterns that reinforce confidence, self-esteem, and value.

Like emotions, if we acknowledge and accept the thought, we allow the thought to settle. We become the observer. "I hear you" or "I feel you" are strong acknowledgments you can tell your inner critic to help dissipate its power of judgment. This offers an opportunity to soothe the inner wounds, by being present and addressing upsets or false beliefs.

When your inner critic is at work, think of it as the voice of your wounded inner child. It's like a tape recorder of the false beliefs and fears developed (or heard) over the years. If we play the recording without conscious thought or attention, we will continue to hear the same thing. Press pause, listen, and accept what you hear, then apply a new script of your truth. This truth becomes real with continued practice. With practice, you become masterful.

Becoming masterful is more than "thinking positive" or making affirmations. Positive thinking is useful to explore higher perspectives, but we need to honor the way we feel and allow our thoughts and feelings to transform healthily. People often use positive thinking as an escape from processing the feelings they need to work through.

It's possible to rewire our emotional nature and wounded selves by applying gentle but firm discipline, including acknowledging false truths, accepting emotions to discern the source of shame and guilt, and taking micro-step actions to apply deep compassion for our humanness.

Another way to heal the inner critic is to take inventory and acknowledge a potential pattern of self-sabotage. What part of you is keeping you stuck in a lower vibrational frequency attached to your old imprints? As you identify the critic, you can shift your energy from judgment to acceptance, and then follow with action. Below are a list of terms to describe different types of inner critics. Choose those you most identify with, and note if certain terms define a pattern in your relationships.

Blamer: Are you mad, angry, accusatory, or otherwise stuck in a loop of looking to blame others for your current mood or outlook?

Critic: Are you critical of your looks, lack of success, your partner's behavior, or comparing yourself to a friend/colleague?

Defender: Do you feel on edge, defensive, or the need to rationalize your feelings or behavior to ensure acceptance from others?

Wounded Child: Do you feel unusually uneasy and off-balance emotionally, stuck in a fear pattern of feeling unsafe, unloved, or unworthy? Are you easily triggered and act out from a place of pain?

Foe: Are you treating yourself unkindly by not taking care of your emotional needs, not eating a healthy diet, not taking risks, making poor choices, or denying yourself compassion?

Fixer: Are you focused on helping others in order to feel a sense of value or worth? Do you make sure others are okay so that you feel okay?

Keep in mind that these terms do not identify you. They are words and phrases to help reveal your inner critic when it attempts to stop you from growth. Revealing your inner critic can help indicate where you need to apply self-love efforts. The pattern that is attached to your inner critic stems from old emotional imprints that developed false beliefs about who you are, therefore limiting your potential. After acknowledging and accepting your patterns, use the following list to guide you into actions of self-love.

Friend: Be kind to yourself and accept your life and emotions as well as what you have to offer. Becoming your own friend is the first action step to heal repetitive patterns.

Forgiver: Open your heart to become loving and offer grace and forgiveness to yourself and those in your presence. Acknowledging your own humanity and trying your best allows room for more self-compassion.

Lover: Being present, tender, and compassionate can allow yourself to feel loved. Do you have a heart full of promise and hope? What goodness can you wish for yourself today and for those you love?

Healer: Taking ownership of your feelings and negative patterns by applying the AAA Method will help attend to the imbalances that arise in your body, mind, or emotions. As you commit to self-growth and have faith in something greater than yourself, you can follow your intuition and lead with your heart to healing.

Let's be clear about the difference between discernment and judgment. Judging is the act of choosing good or bad or right or wrong. It often comes from the inner critic who is either projecting pain or trying to avoid more pain. The mind attempts to avoid discomfort by averting attempts to grow, change, or take risks. This is especially true for risks that could discredit false beliefs that you are unworthy, when in fact, with new skills you would realize that you are worthy. Your mind does not want you to suffer, it just doesn't have the emotional or spiritual intelligence that you have.

You are not your mind. If you rely on your mind to control your behavior, you will indeed be held back by its limited abilities to override false beliefs. This is why we work on emotions and energy. You must retrain your mind to know that you are safe to grow, that new patterns can be healthy, and that when you feel differently, you will think differently. In this case the word *differently* means more than feeling happy, sad, or angry. It means vibrational differences. Energy is important, and can effect a positive shift in our mental and emotional bodies. It is all connected.

Whereas judgment is of the mind, discernment is of a higher wisdom. Discernment uses our senses to get a clearer vision of what is true and real. Although discernment and judgment seem closely related, discernment is a healthier choice (a higher vibration) that is connected to conscious mindfulness, rather than to reactionary beliefs from the limited mind. Discernment needs our higher minds to see, versus the limited mind to critique.

Discerning (tuning into our feelings instead of reacting with our minds and egos to old stories) also provides stability for emotional processing. We have a wonderful opportunity to level up to our divine nature and heal our limited beliefs. Discernment is a high vibrational ability, and needs a foundation of self-trust, self-confidence, and connection to your higher self.

As you practice self-love and raising your vibration in the days to come, act as a detective to discern your actions, thoughts, and patterns and notice who is showing up in your life each day. Write about these discernments in your journal each evening in the third person. First identify the person who showed up (the Blamer, Critic, Defender, Wounded Child, Foe, or Fixer). Imagine what this person says to your best friend. List and observe their woes, their judgments of self and others, who they blame, and why they are defensive. As you listen to your story through this voice, imagine how you would counsel them. What do you hear them saying and what do you see as their pattern or issue? It may look something like this:

> She is so hard on herself today. She takes on so much responsibility and doesn't give herself a break. I see an insecurity that is seemingly uncalled for, although it must be from a past hurt, likely related to her father being so hard on her. She's a lovely woman, although it appears that she doesn't recognize it, because she is scorning the size of her legs. She's angry at her spouse and criticizing him. Maybe she isn't appreciating the qualities of herself enough or she has too high expectations of him or what he doesn't give her. No one

is confirming her insecurities at the moment, so I assume this judgment is coming from an old trigger that makes her think she isn't good enough. I guess it is related to the comments her friend's mother made that she "couldn't see her knees" the day she wore shorts in middle school.

Notice how you spoke to yourself about who you are. If you have a hard time remembering or catching the internal dialogue, set a reminder on your computer or phone that says "What did you just say?" to prompt a mindfulness to your inner voice.

Next, apply the AAA Method in your journal writing using the above guide, friend, forgiver, lover, and healer. Writing again in the third person, as if you were talking to a friend, see if you can help soothe your inner critic by offering presence (friendships), forgiveness (self-compassion), love (encouragement and validation), and healing (acknowledgement, acceptance, and action). It may look something like this:

I see you struggling with insecurity today and being hard on yourself. I know it must be hard to juggle so much, there's a lot of stress to manage. I'm here for you and love you so much. I see your legs and they are healthy and strong. Many would love to walk in your shoes. Be gentle with yourself and take the time you need to process those deep hurts. It's hard to remember sometimes, but your friend's mother had her own insecurities and insensitivities. Her comment really had nothing to do with you. Part of healing is recognizing other's limitations and not taking things so personally, but looking at what can be done internally. You are such a sweet and beautiful person, lovable too! Why don't you take some time doing something kind and healthy like a nice walk and deep breathing? Maybe listen to that favorite band of yours too. That always puts a smile on your face and a lightness in your step!

Finding Compassion

Compassion and forgiveness are two basic emotions that can be difficult to give to ourselves if we have experienced years of neglect and pain. Tapping into these energies requires a committed persistence. When you may not feel forgiving, apply the presence of self-love. Even when you feel confused about what compassion feels like, take actions to show yourself that you care.

Compassion is care in action. It's an emotion that is full of awareness and acceptance, blended with behaviors that relay information of love. Think of a helpless young pup, or a child who is down and out. When you feel compassion for someone, the natural inclination is to offer help, even if that's offering a hug, a cup of tea, a listening ear, or trying to cheer someone up. We sympathize and we have that tug in our hearts that feels deeply for a person in need. When it's you that's hurting, can you feel deeply for yourself, or your inner child? Can you hold the space for the pain, be present, and extend loving kindness?

Self-care is what we must offer ourselves. If you feel undeserving, it's likely that you are stuck in old energetic imprints of shame, guilt, or fear. The inability to forgive is a signal to apply the AAA Method. Practice this Method until you feel neutral, and then take microsteps toward self-love. This will help you feel worthy, and that you can trust yourself in the face of difficult situations or triggers.

Displaying gratitude is one of the easiest ways to tap into forgiveness and compassion. It's difficult to remain in fear, anger, or shame when you connect with things for which you are grateful.

> "Gratitude makes sense of our past, brings peace for today, and creates a vision for tomorrow."
> —Melody Beattie, author of *Codependent No More*

Take a quick break to become present. List three to four things you feel grateful for today. Don't itemize the things you "should" feel grateful for. Practice feeling grateful for things that bring you relief, joy, satisfaction, hope, or whatever opens your heart. Lists are effective reminders when you feel stuck. They're an easy way to quickly increase your energy vibration.

Sending Love

There doesn't ever seem to be enough time to do what we want and need to accomplish. The reality is that progress toward self-love and healing may not happen quickly. Take time and challenge yourself with the task below.

Get a piece of paper and an envelope. If you have stationery, that's even better. At the top of the paper, write your name, followed by a comma. I want you to write a love letter to yourself. The letter should speak to the self-sabotage, self-harm, criticisms, and anguish you have experienced. Using the tools in this book, be reminded that hope is possible. Practice the AAA Method. Reinforce your truths and strengths. Most importantly, offer as much compassion and forgiveness for yourself as possible, and state it in words. Write how sorry you feel for ignoring your needs. How grateful you are to have a new opportunity for forgiveness and self-love. Relate your love for your innocent inner child. Convey your anguish for the negative words and behaviors you experience in order to protect yourself, then practice forgiveness. Open your heart and make amends to someone you truly love.

When you complete this letter of love, forgiveness, and understanding, place the letter in the envelope and mail it to yourself. Use a stamp and drop it at the post office. You are worth the time and effort!

Honoring Your Worth

There are many ways to interpret the world that could confirm negative thoughts stemming from emotional imprints such as "I am not worth anyone's time, money, friendship, or love." Seeking that confirmation does not make it true, it serves to activate the core wounds from traumatic childhood experiences. As you continue on the path of healing, it is up to you to stop this false belief cycle based on other people's words, wounds, and shortcomings.

Understanding your worth starts with acknowledging the truth of who you are, accepting your previous story (who you believed yourself to be in relation to others or who others believe you should be), and taking action to love yourself. Loving yourself builds self-confidence, self-worth, trust, balance, and inner peace. It is a beautiful thing.

Take notice when the voice of negative self-talk, criticism, or shame begins. The voice may be small or large but is part of your self-love language. It wants to keep you attached to the fear of false truths that you are not enough. Also notice when your inner voice says, "yeah, but . . ."

Try to answer these questions with love and appreciation without any excuses or judgment. Write the answers in your journal.

What do you value most about your body?
(Example: I love and appreciate the way my body heals itself. Sometimes when I am sick or have a cut on my skin, I'm amazed at how my body performs and heals itself. It makes me want to care for my body even more.)

What do you value most about your personality or character?
(Example: I love that I am flexible, diverse, and have an adventurous spirit. When I am in the flow of life and trusting myself I am an outgoing person who loves to explore and enjoy the company of other people. I love to help people and that feels wonderful.)

What do you value most about your mind?
(Example: I value that my mind wants to keep learning. I love to observe people, and experience new things. The fact that I can continue to take in information and process it amazes me!)

115

What do you value most about your emotions?
(Example: I am a very sensitive and emotional person. I value the fact that I can feel my feelings, and I have access to a wide range of emotions. I appreciate that I cry easily when I feel sad or afraid and also have the emotional resources to understand the difference between my emotions.)

The more we acknowledge, accept, and openly share about the qualities that make us the amazing people we are, the more we shift the inner voice of the critic to a voice that speaks praise, confidence, and love to our inner child. It is a powerful way to shift energetic imprints. The feelings that come with appreciation, compassion, acceptance, and grace alert your inner self that you are beautiful, unique, and special. You are so gifted and capable, worthy and valuable.

Have you ever stopped to think how blessed you are to have your body, the tiny hairs, the functioning lungs, the magical way your organs function and keep you alive? You are truly a miracle! How can you be a miracle and not be worthy? It's just not possible.

Buying-Power Exercise

We've now come to one of my favorite self-love exercises. This exercise is about honoring your worth. Think of one of your favorite people. This should be a person you like to shower with affection, love, gifts, and goodness. (You aren't allowed to change the person when you read the exercise!)

What would you gift them for their birthday or holiday? How do you show your love and bring joy to their life? Do you go out of your way to get an item or create a special experience? Do you save up money to splurge on their special day? Do you take time off to help them celebrate an important life event? As soon as possible, purchase something of similar cost to what you would gift your loved one or spend the same energy to create an experience for them, but do this for yourself. No excuses.

You may feel your insides recoil. You're thinking of all the reasons why you "shouldn't" or why you "can't." This exercise helps to wrestle with the belief that you don't matter *as much*. That you don't *need* something. That you aren't worth the expense of a gift that isn't *necessary*.

As mentioned earlier in this book, it's not necessary to spend money to experience self-love. Money is often a superficial expression. But this is a practice to help you look into the feelings you have about yourself. Do you overspend on yourself but are stingy with others? Do you only spend on others and not yourself? What comes to mind when given the direction to create an experience that honors yourself, no matter the effort, time, or cost? Take a moment to delve into any lingering false beliefs that say you are not as valuable as others or that you don't deserve joy. You are worth as much time, energy, and love as any other being on earth.

Chapter 7
Create Healthy Boundaries

🌱

THERE are many ways to encourage self-growth and confidence. One of the most impactful ways is to establish and implement healthy boundaries within relationships. If you struggle to feel inner strength and/or trust in yourself and others, creating boundaries will give you the supportive structure to move forward.

Your needs matter just as much as another's, and creating boundaries is a personal step toward healing. Boundaries can be difficult to establish and maintain if you have negative belief patterns stemming from former wounds and emotional imprints. Some may fear that implementing boundaries would be hurtful and ultimately lead to rejection. Saying no can bring up insecurities that make us think we do not have a place of worth to have a voice. Or we fear that defining our needs would cause strife within the family or intimate relationships.

It's important to know that these fears may arise when considering boundaries, but applying the AAA Method will help move you past them. It's also important to understand the difference between unhealthy and healthy boundaries. Unhealthy boundaries serve as protective walls created out of the need to protect, defend, or keep others at bay. Healthy boundaries serve to establish deeper intimacy, trust, and a sense of personal safety, allowing better relationships with others.

The Walls We Build

Let's look at the emotional and energetic walls we build and how they differ from healthy boundaries. Emotional walls are thoughts or energy put forth to help avoid future pain from others. These walls are defense mechanisms to provide a sense of "safety," but ultimately, they create separation from our authentic selves, and keep us in a self-destructive mindset. The emotional walls we build are often subconscious limits on our feelings or experiences in an effort to avoid more hurt. Some people make conscious decisions to limit experiences, but this behavior limits joy rather than keeping negative feelings out. Have you ever had any of these thoughts?

- "That's the last time I'll ever do that."
- "I need to protect my heart."
- "I'll never go through that kind of pain again."
- "Men/women can't be trusted."
- "I gave it all I had and it didn't work, so I'm not trying again."

These types of reactions are based in fear. To avoid past hurt or rejection, we build mental walls to limit pain by blocking opportunities and love. Most people don't desire to block love or good feelings, but that's what happens when we control experiences to limit pain.

Shifting our mindset from avoidance to allowance will heal our hearts and create healthier relationships. Allowance doesn't mean allowing others to take advantage of us. Nor does it mean we allow negative patterns or people who vibrate at a low level to pull us down to our previous emotional imprints. Allowance is being open to full experiences in your life. As you learn healthy boundaries and how to trust in yourself, it will become easier to handle experiences in new and more positive ways.

Transcending the Walls in Your Heart

Some people believe that in order to heal we must dismantle the emotional walls by tearing them down one experience at a time to replace every personal thought, feeling, or memory. That is an exhausting and impractical process. If too much time is spent analyzing how the walls were built, we will lack the energy needed to implement healthier structures.

Life and healing are not linear events. The effort to figure out actions and emotions from the past results in looking back at others, rather than looking forward within. In remodeling a kitchen, we remove each tile, trash it, and put in a new one. But as emotional beings, a multidimensional approach is more effective in remodeling our lives. With the higher intelligence of our consciousness and emotional brains, we are capable of holding space for the past as well as the now, all while creating a dynamic future.

When fear, pain, or lower vibrational energy is present due to unhealthy past experiences, the heart can be difficult to open, fearing the risk of vulnerability. Yet we are emotionally intelligent beings, so we crave and need love and connection even when we can't acknowledge that need.

It's tempting to control the flow and exchange of love in an attempt to monitor potential threats. For example, some people become excellent "givers," always outpouring help, energy, love, and gifts. Being a giving person is a beautiful quality, but over-giving is a defense mechanism and a distraction from personal needs. The heart becomes a one-way street, allowing the giver to experience part of the love exchange, but blocks love from being accepted within to avoid potential pain. If you give but don't receive, you may have created walls to prevent being hurt in your relationships.

Others operate differently, opening their heart to receive love, but closing their heart to give love. This type of behavior is often diagnosed as narcissistic, but in reality it is behavior by those hiding behind a fear of unworthiness. True narcissists may have a wound in deep shame, which manifests as ego-based but is actually insecurity. Perhaps those with insecurities were shut down or denied by a parent, or made to feel that what they offered wasn't good enough. This results in an emotional imprint manifested as behavioral limitations projected by the ego.

If only parts of our hearts are open, we limit the fullness of love and create a roller-coaster addiction pattern, and often a back-and-forth power exchange in relationships. This is one way to self-destruct in an emotional way that can lead to the experience of love feeling heavy, controlled, and manipulated. For example, you may have experienced a difficult breakup or loss. The pain was excruciating and in the process of grief, you decided (subconsciously or consciously) to not go through a similar experience again. The pain was too big and you decided not to risk the heartbreak again. So you closed down your heart and limited when or if you would love again, instead of being open to see what new love experience may come in the future.

In this example, we stop co-creating our life from an empowered place of trust and intuition, and limit most possibilities from approaching us. This could also lead to attracting others who operate on a similar vibrational level. Two people with walls in place will stress their relationship within the tension of those walls.

It's tempting to shut down or turn off the part of us that was hurt, but love cannot operate healthily this way. A closed heart limits intimacy, trust, vulnerability, and authenticity. We are always on guard. If we pick and choose the part of our heart and experiences to keep, we must turn away the rest. This causes a constant state of internal conflict, damaging our psyche, emotional bodies, relationships, and energy field. In a state of conflict, we cannot raise our vibration.

Fear

I was dating this person and we were having a very difficult time. I couldn't understand what the issues were, so I talked with my therapist. She said, "Remember, when a person fully opens their heart, it is not all rainbows and sunshine that come out. The pain, unresolved grief, and fear come out too." With her counsel I gained insight into the heart of the other person, but it also made sense of my own fears as I walked toward another relationship that could potentially hurt me. I felt tinges of love, excitement, and hope, but I also felt threatened by pain and grief from my past.

Because these past feelings can be overwhelming, it's important to slowly open our hearts, and boundaries can be helpful. Take small steps to open your heart to see more of the world, or dip your toe into a new relationship, while making sure you always feel safe. All of this requires that we not become a victim to our previous pain, but honor it by learning from it. It means paying attention to the process.

Admittedly, I have rushed into things and not honored the process at times. The repercussions of rushing can be brutal. Love, just like healing, is a process. Some people meet and fall in love in ten minutes, believing they've found their soul mate. If that's true, they probably learned how to set healthy boundaries. Another possible scenario is that they found someone who vibrated on the same level of emotional imprints and dove into the "perfect match." As you begin to observe yourself from a new and different perspective with a higher frequency, you will feel safe to test new experiences and take a chance in trusting your heart.

Issues of building emotional walls apply to more than intimate relationships. Walls are created with our colleagues, neighbors, friends, and families. It's how we learn to interact with the world out of fear. The goal is to identify these walls and be honest and courageous enough to rise above them to instill healthy boundaries.

Transcendence

Transcendence is to rise above. To best use your energy and efforts (and create new emotional imprints), practice going beyond the mentality that you can change your past or other people, and direct your energy higher. Transcendence is a stepladder to take you beyond the pain and fear, and closer to your higher self. As you transcend, you will experience an immediate positive shift in vibration as you focus on possibility, hope, and growth. Transcendence is the way to awaken a higher perspective.

Transcendence embodies the spirit of acceptance and compassion while helping you rise like a phoenix from the ashes. No longer will you deny your past, but use your energy to create the future. The story that held you back can be integrated into your present being, creating fullness and experience without triggering you and dragging you down. Allow your heart to open. Allow the exchange of love to flow openly both ways as a receiver and a giver. Be confident that love is a medicine to heal as it releases harmful fears. With healthy and strong boundaries, you can rise above and operate safely in your heart space, body, and mind.

Healthy Boundaries

Establishing emotional boundaries is important to achieving good mental health. Boundaries are crucial for healthy intimate relationships, but also very important for family, friends, and work relationships. Additionally, healthy boundaries can expand the possibilities of intimacy.

Emotional health and growth require clear boundaries. The fear of declaring boundaries is that by creating self-care measures it will lead to rejection or aloneness. These fears stem from our emotional imprints, triggering a low vibration. Healthy boundaries expand the possibilities of intimacy and trust in all relationships and offer more emotional availability with your partner. It's helpful to think of healthy boundaries as the opposite of emotional walls. We do not create them to limit our experience or feelings, but to expand the possibility of safely feeling, living authentically, and being intimate.

Personally, healthy boundaries have been hard for me to maintain in the past, and may be hard for you too. I continue to practice, and that's all I'm asking of you. It's easy as an authority to tell people how things are done, but the part of me that is eager to help is equally eager to put the work in myself. Regardless of where you fall on building boundaries, know that you are not alone. Boundaries are hard to enforce, but they can make the difference between a toxic relationship and a healthy one.

Why are boundaries hard to enforce? Some people with certain emotional imprints fear their boundaries will hurt the feelings of others. They fear rejection if they assert what they want and need. The fear is similar to being left alone on an island, with a fortress barrier that no one can penetrate because they are "too much" or "intolerable." Fortunately, this is not true.

Some people use boundaries as an opportunity to assert authority, control others, or get revenge. These reasons stem from an addiction to pain and cannot sustain healthy boundaries. Seeking authority, control, or revenge is tied to a feeling of pain. Healthy boundaries provide guidance on how to operate, create safety, and show ourselves respect. They are very effective tools for clear communication and they offer a deep sense of trust. This is true for us personally, as well as for other people.

Within the family, healthy boundaries can be challenging, especially if family members act as victims or pile on guilt. As you grow up and become a responsible adult, family members may try to "make you feel" responsible for their happiness and well-being, or to manage their emotional needs. Do not try to control or fix the lives of others. And do not expect others to fix your life. That's why boundaries are helpful. Putting boundaries in place will help you break up with blame and take ownership of your life. No longer a victim, martyr, or blamer, boundaries help to define your time, ownership, and space.

You may think, *But I'm my mom's best friend and if I spend too much time involved in my life, she'll be lonely and upset. I want to find my friend a better job so she stops complaining about money and we can go on vacations together. I need to help my stepdaughter care for her kids because I have more experience and I can see she's struggling. My boyfriend tells me what to wear and although it makes me uncomfortable, I don't want him to feel insecure or jealous when we're out.* Mom needs her own friends and happiness, and you need to live your own life without guilt or shame. Your friend is responsible for finding her own job and making the money she feels she deserves, wants, or needs. It's her choice to prioritize a vacation. Your stepdaughter needs to practice being a mom and only asking for help and support when she needs it. You need to decide what clothes make you feel comfortable and respectable, and let your boyfriend work through his insecurities and improve his self-esteem. He should not ask you to protect his fears.

It is hard to watch a parent or sibling suffer. If others ask for your help and you can assist them without jeopardizing your own life or breaking your boundaries, helping is a gift. But it isn't your responsibility to take care of the emotional well-being of others, or the financial cares of those who are capable. It's not your job to make your mom happy, or your father less lonely. You cannot change their feelings. You can only give love and understanding.

There are times you may want to spend more time with your father, or take your sister's children for the weekend, or feel compassion for your boyfriend. There's nothing wrong with that, but make sure you are doing these things because you want to, not because you feel obligated or fear someone will leave you if you decline. Creating healthy boundaries ahead of time will help you determine the right course of action for you.

Children also need boundaries, discipline, and support to learn and to grow. They actually crave structure to help them understand expectations, privacy, and respect of social norms. Children with healthy boundaries learn what is right and wrong and how to function within appropriate behaviors. They know that stepping outside of those boundaries results in repercussions. Over time, they understand tolerance, trust, responsibility, and respect. They also know how to interact with their parents and siblings in an intimate way.

The same is true for adults.

Firm boundaries help bring clarity to the needs that best serve your highest good. Start by asking for what you need, speaking your truth, and not relying on others to take care of your emotional needs. With this understanding, others will find it easier to relate to you.

If you feel extra stress or fear during a chaotic time in life, try to enforce more boundaries, including alone time such as carving out time to take online courses or meditate. To set a new boundary, alert your mate that you need more time or space to take care of yourself. Not taking care of yourself and turning on Netflix will avoid your needs, playing into the addiction of self-sabotage.

The structure of healthy boundaries helps us to show up, be fully present, and develop true intimacy with ourselves. We don't cling or feel needy when we're fulfilling our own inner needs with self-care and strong boundaries in place. Healthy boundaries not only protect your needs, they also place value on your worth and integrity.

Healthy boundaries put a kibosh on unhealthy attachments, dysfunctional partnerships, abusive family members, or codependent friends. Wouldn't it be amazing to be free of unhealthy interactions and relationships? You can create that world if you choose. When we are stuck in unhealthy patterns and dependencies it can seem impossible to break free, but it is possible using the AAA Method. Acknowledgment, acceptance, and action with an added dose of courage and commitment can help you break the cycle.

Boundaries are more than just saying no, although that can be a part of your boundary language if needed. It's also about saying yes to what you do need, and learning to function within the space of clear expectations. It may be true that the person you have certain expectations from cannot satisfy your needs. In this case, it is time to reevaluate if this is a healthy expectation from a partner, or if you can accept them for who they are.

If you fear boundaries, there may be more work to do with your inner child. Perhaps he/she still feels afraid of being left, unprotected, unworthy, or invalidated. Remind your inner child that he/she is strong, capable, and healthy, and that you don't need validation or approval from anyone other than your adult self. We all need healthy love, but it truly starts inside of us. Boundaries are a wonderful self-love tool. It's important that you review your boundaries as you continue to heal to be sure they remain in alignment with your higher self.

What do boundaries look like? Here are a few examples:

- No work texts after 6:00 pm.
- Taking one day of personal space away from your partner each month.
- No calls from family before noon or after 8:00 pm (unless an emergency).
- Not to be spoken to in a diminishing way by your boss.
- A thirty-minute speaking break after an argument.
- One month of dating before intimacy.
- A special savings account for future night classes that only you can access.
- No conversations about politics or news at dinner.
- Being able to say "I'm sorry, I'm not able to help you with that" when your brother asks for regular nonpaid childcare.
- Saying yes to something you desire.

Once you have healthy boundaries in place you can more easily accept people for who they are, free from trying to be someone you are not in order to accommodate others. Should they need your support, let them ask and then determine what feels right to you. This is easier when the people you are in relationships with also have healthy boundaries and self-care practices. If not, perhaps you can be a healthy example for them.

The most difficult part about implementing boundaries is enforcing them. You are the only gatekeeper, so it's up to you to follow through on what you need. If someone crosses the boundary and there are no repercussions, you don't have a boundary, you have a suggestion. If fear keeps you from saying or doing something to protect your boundary, you need to reframe how shame, guilt, fear, and disappointment are controlling your life.

If your boundary is crossed, make a plan to follow through with action. This may include a conversation (speaking your truth), other communication (an email, setting a meeting with a counselor), taking space, and/or deciding when and how to resolve the matter that is fair to both parties. You can still have forgiveness, compassion, and love while maintaining boundaries. They simply offer healthy ways to secure a safe space in your life, and in your future. If the boundary is to be respected, be consistent and follow through with legitimate self-care steps that honor those boundaries every day, particularly during times of stress, crises, or global pandemics.

When you confidently ask for what you need, speak your truth, and do not rely on others to take care of your emotional needs, it's possible to gain the bandwidth to relate in a healthier way because you feel safe to fully be present. From a safe place, learn to trust and be vulnerable and intimate with others. There is no need to be clingy or feel needy, because you are fulfilling your inner needs. There is no fear of abuse because guidelines (boundaries) are in place to alert you before abuse can start, or continue.

When others are allowed to treat us poorly, do not blame them because you are the one allowing it. The guilt-trips, the shaming, or the lies—none of that is about you, it's about them, but you've taken it on as a means to enforce your own lower vibrational pattern. Without clear boundaries, you give poor treatment permission to become a part of your life. Always check to see if you are operating from a place of guilt, shame, codependency, or false beliefs that you are not worthy when inside an unhealthy relationship. Abusive patterns can be stopped. You cannot control the actions of others, for that is not your responsibility. But you can control your own.

We abandon ourselves when others are allowed to cross our boundaries or when we don't honor our personal boundaries. These actions take us back to the addiction to pain we feel when we think we don't matter. When your needs are abandoned, your inner child

OVERCOMING TOXIC EMOTIONS

gets triggered and you begin to operate from a lower vibrational imprint.

What boundaries do you need? In your journal, practice writing boundaries for specific people and situations. For example, you may title one page "work." What boundaries do you need with your boss or colleagues? Some examples may be:

- Allow text exchanges between 8:00 am–6:00 pm only.
- Respond to emails up until 7:00 pm only.
- Log off of work devices at 8:00 pm.
- Do not work through lunch breaks.
- Ask to be spoken to in a respectful way.

Write your boundaries and remember to focus only on what you need. Don't fixate on what you don't need, as that can stir up defenses. Include how you will handle situations if your boundaries are broken. Make a boundary page for each person or situation in which you may need to implement safe structure.

One of my favorite quotes is from Brené Brown, "Being clear is being kind." When we don't speak with clear intention, authenticity, feelings, or thoughts, we are not giving the other person the opportunity to care for us fully or respect our boundaries. And that's not fair or kind to either party. We cannot expect others to know what we need or who we are unless we clearly tell them. When we speak with clarity, even when it's difficult, we honor the other person, and we respect their emotional intelligence and capability. Being clear offers opportunities to give and receive care, own our worth, and acknowledge the worth of others. It is a kind and clean way to relate.

If we don't know who we are, what we want or need, or how to emotionally care for ourselves, being clear is impossible. It's vitally important to work through the steps of discovering who you are versus who you thought you were in relation to others (See Chapters 2 and 3 on pages 25 and 53). Understanding yourself is the foundation for self-care. When you are clear about how you feel, who you are, and learn to take emotional care of yourself, you will be happier, stronger, and living a life you truly love.

Transcending-the-Walls Meditation

The following mindfulness meditation is a five-minute practice intended to help you observe your inner world. With intention, this practice can be very profound. This is an excellent time to practice the AAA Method.

Close your eyes and begin to focus on your breath. Follow your breath into your body, allowing your muscles to relax. Your breathing is effortless. Place full intention on your inhalation and imagine your breath traveling down into your belly and becoming one with your rhythmic flow. Begin sensing your internal organs, tapping into your inner landscape, emotions, muscles, bones, and circulation. If you feel anxious, small, sad, or disempowered, sit with that and breathe acceptance into your heart until it softens. This can be the action step toward healing, sitting and breathing, being the observer of your experience.

With your inner voice, ask yourself where you have constructed emotional walls or blocks in your heart or physical body. Listen closely for any messages, resistance, anger, tears, or revelations. You may also ask yourself, what purpose do these walls serve?

Imagine with each inhale that your breath elevates you to a higher place. You become lighter, freer, and you see your world with a new perspective. Each inhale allows you to make space for all of your history and difficulty, while continuing to rise stronger, more capable and accepting. Put a smile on your face while you breathe. Feel your body integrate your past experiences while also expanding to create new life.

When you are ready, use your exhales to begin grounding yourself in the current moment. Before coming out of meditation, make sure you feel safe and grounded. Take your time and use your senses to notice the smells and feelings in your current room. When you are ready, gently open your eyes.

Meditation can be challenging, but the beauty of meditation is that there is no right or wrong. It's about being in the moment of the experience. Just doing it is doing it right! These aren't easy things to move through, so be proud of your efforts.

Chapter 8
Free Emotions and Find Stability

IT'S important to always remember that your mind is strong, but it's also important to know that your heart is stronger. The power is within you to change your life. By learning about your emotions and doing the work to heal, you are making conscious and brave efforts toward self-love to meet the highest vibration of your soul. You are evolving and changing with every breath you take. With every thought and every recognized emotion, you are rising up into your highest alignment. You are love.

One of the greatest lessons in life is to learn that pain and love are coexisting emotions. This is the human condition. With practice, we can come to acknowledge and respect the relationship between love and pain, and learn that this is the most fragile yet strongest force of nature.

Every day, think about how love in action is the ultimate compassion. Reading books may not change your life, but the commitment to learn reinforces a new self-love language that will improve your vibration and create a new imprint, filled with beliefs that are yours, and emotions that are healthier. Learning new information can open you to new possibilities. Be proud of your efforts and commitment. You are giving a gift to yourself and to the world.

Personal growth can become stymied when people become overwhelmed. When we get overwhelmed, it's difficult to take action. It's easy to focus on the big picture of your life and forget what is available right now. Healing personal trauma or deeply ingrained belief patterns requires you to acknowledge and accept your past, while remaining present in the now with intention to create change. Utilizing the AAA Method will help you refocus and build a sustainable foundation, while also attending to the pain of past experiences.

When feeling overwhelmed in a situation, pause and remove yourself from the situation as gently as possible, whether excusing yourself to the restroom or saying "I need a moment." Take a breath, and while thinking of the particular problem or relationship in your life, apply the AAA Method.

AAA Method

Acknowledge the feeling, behavior, or dynamic in the relationship and recognize if this is a recurring pattern, a trigger for your inner child, or an addiction to emotional imprints.

Accept the feeling and situation so that you can own your part.

Act by taking micro-steps toward a new vibrational experience that is sustainable.

Some people think that our thoughts are stronger than our emotions, but it is really the other way around. The search for mental clarity, mental stability, acuity, and peace is a driving force behind quests for healing. A common misperception is if we fix our minds, we make ourselves right. Using knowledge and analyzing our processes is fine, but don't ignore addictions to emotional responses and how they will set us up for repeated patterns.

There are generally two types of people: thinker types who analyze and rationalize everything in their lives, and emotional types who experience the world by their feelings, throwing lists out the window. Balance is important regardless of your type. We are naturally inclined to process emotions, but the impact of negative emotional wounds compels many of us to function from our minds.

If you are a more rational, logical person by nature, it is helpful to learn skills to access your emotions. It's not always what you think, but what you feel. In your daily language, notice the words you use to describe your experience. Do you use more "I think" or "I feel" statements?

People who function with their mind too often get caught up with the whirlwind of information and speed of communication transmission, so they spend most of their time trying to understand and rationalize with worry, overthinking, or judgment. They disregard other types of intelligence such as their heart, intuition, or energy to make decisions.

Everyone has access to emotion, but many ignore emotional intelligence and rely on their minds to make sense of the world. As every thought has a feeling attached to it, it makes sense to place our efforts toward exploring the feeling of our experiences, rather than attempting to only make rational sense of it. This action puts us in touch with our subtle senses such as energy and intuition, and helps us gain a greater awareness of our vibrational shifts in environments and relationships.

Many intelligent people have not developed the emotional intelligence or sensitivity to live from their higher vibrational self. Mental intelligence does not equate to emotional health. Nor does it enhance our peace of mind, intuition, or individual perspectives. The path to spiritual awakening and self-realization doesn't happen by becoming smarter or more analytical. This evolution takes a different kind of wisdom.

One of my former clients is a successful brain surgeon with a reputation of saving people's lives. He is keenly aware of how the brain functions and the protocol to help patients through dire emergencies. His career was thriving, but personally he was miserable. He struggled his entire life with a deep sense of shame, which hindered his ability to enjoy healthy relationships. He used money to solve problems, and he ignored issues with potential partners because he ignored his emotional wounds and the need to heal them.

It is possible to use various energy patterns in various situations. At work a person may vibrate at a higher level than in their personal lives or vice versa. This is due to the type of wounding and severity of our wounds. One may connect and excel in the workplace if they are confident and talented at their craft, allowing the mind and ego to accomplish the task at hand. In relationships, they may carry out an emotional imprint that says they are unlovable or unworthy. Without achieving personal growth, they are stuck in a lower vibrational pattern that causes stress, anxiety, and unhappiness.

Fear of feeling hinders access to emotional intelligence. It may feel safer to think our way through our lives rather than feeling our way through, but this behavior only feeds the fear of feeling. It is scary to look at the fear of pain or loss in the face. The lack of acknowledgment and acceptance of a loss disconnects us from our main power source—love. Instead, we experience fragmented mental and emotional lives. It's not possible to force truths or untruths without causing psychological damage. Attempting to make an experience untrue in your emotional body may cause long-term mental, emotional, or physical disease. Heartbreak has stimulated physical ailments and addictions, and lingering grief or anger can last a lifetime, sometimes shortening one's life. Our minds try to protect us from feeling pain, so it diverts pain to anxiety, denial, magical thinking, or other avenues of mental escape and dissociation. We use our minds as a first line of defense.

It's not possible to control the amount of pain or suffering we will experience in our lifetime, but processing and managing how we intake experiences can lead to freedom and long-term stability. By coming to full acknowledgment and acceptance, you can allow your mind to be an observer without dominating your action. Take micro-steps to increase self-confidence so that you can be the facilitator in processing your emotions.

Some time ago, my inner critic was shaming me about sleeping late. I felt like a lazy child and was thankful that I was living alone so no one could witness my faults. I reverted to a mental defense mode and self-sabotage as I created rationalizations and excuses for my behavior. But I continued to feel like a failure. I tried to find self-compassion, but it didn't work because I was dealing with both a mental false belief (there's only a certain time to wake up that is acceptable for adults) and an emotional belief (I am unworthy, I feel like a fraud).

I felt compelled to explain to my parents, to clients, and to God why I was sleeping later and not beginning my workday until noon. Even as I write now, I feel the need to explain the insomnia caused by peri-menopause, or how I have to catch my cat late at night, or my blue-light addiction due to writing this book, or the adrenal over-load from moving to a new town, alone, during a pandemic. (But, I won't.)

AAA Method

I **acknowledged** the reasons I've been sleeping late.

I fully **accepted** my behavior, and assured my inner child that I don't think any less of her for trying to get the rest she needs. I told myself that there's no shame in keeping different hours than other people, and I reminded myself how fortunate it is to be able to create my own schedule.

I developed an **action** plan of micro-steps to encourage better sleep hygiene: more water each day, turning off the computer before 9:00 pm, daily exercise, and herbal support for hormones.

Eventually, I stopped and thought, *Hold-up, Leah, you are feeling triggered and small. Utilize the AAA Method.* With the knowledge learned from the Method, I moved from my self-deprecating state and into the present state of an adult with tools to help me improve.

I no longer felt shame. I was empowered, and I looked forward to retiring each night as early as possible, even if just a few minutes earlier than before. Perhaps you can relate to this story. This process may seem exhaustive, but all of those thoughts happened within seconds. It's awareness and commitment that can bring us to the moment when our vibration quickly shifts from shame to self-confidence. Feeling like a child, I was resonating the vibration of a three to a four that was associated with my emotional imprint of shame. I wanted to hide in a closet, but after processing and applying the Method, my vibration improved to a seven or eight, and I went on with my day. You can achieve similar results with practice. Don't deny yourself. Be an active observer of your thoughts and emotions and use your power to create change.

Perspective

The ability to understand and acquire emotional freedom requires a change in perspective. Emotional imprints and belief systems were developed over time according to the information and behaviors we witnessed and absorbed from those around us. With conscious thought, it's possible to move to a higher perspective and gain not only understanding, but compassion and peace. Prayer, meditation, and developmental self-care work is very helpful in becoming more grounded.

Referring back to my sleep example, the emotional imprints I developed as a child led me to believe that confident and successful people rise early to get a fresh start to their day. Why do I have these thoughts? I recall feeling ashamed if I slept late, as if I disappointed my mom and dad. I believed they would think less of me if I didn't rise when they did to start my day. My parents, like many others, had obligations and jobs, along with two children, which meant a full day of important things to accomplish. They did what they had to do. Observing this, but also wanting to sleep in or stay up late to play, made me feel that I wasn't responsible or good enough. I was a sensitive child who felt shame if I disappointed my parents.

This belief system surrounding sleep has stayed with me throughout my adult life. Although I know it may be healthier to fall asleep and rise earlier, is it realistic for most people? If you don't follow that schedule, are you a bad person? For years, my answer was yes, and I judged others who slept the morning away. I didn't realize when I was growing up that some people stay up to make art, or have different schedules because of evening work shifts, or chose to enjoy the quiet hours of the dark rather than the early morning sun.

It's easy to judge our actions as "right" or "wrong." It's more difficult to seek self-understanding and acceptance of what is right for our own lives based not on justifications that keep our fears alive and vibrations low, but on what nourishes our higher self.

When I was older I stayed the night at my mom's house and was amazed that she slept until after 9:00 am. It upended my entire belief system and I began to question my previous reality! That instance led me to a new perspective and helped me question my false belief. I realized how limited my mind was when operating from a place of insecurities and self-criticism. My judgmental mind blocked the curious spirit of my heart.

To raise your perspective, use the AAA Method. When we achieve a higher perspective it's possible to put ourselves in someone else's shoes, employing empathy for others and compassion for ourselves. Remember, judgments come from fear in the mind.

People have small views of the world from their lens of limited beliefs and fear. Being curious and having compassion and acceptance allows one to step outside of lower vibrations and view the world from a higher place. As an example, Joe the sculptor likes to work in the evening when it is cooler and more quiet in the house. He sleeps during the morning hours and he and his family accept his preferred schedule. Joe is clear about who he is, and with perspective

AAA Method

Acknowledge false beliefs by calling them out.

Accept that these beliefs have been with you for a long time, even though they make you uncomfortable or bring conflict.

Act to take micro-steps in discovering what is true for you. Ask yourself *Is this true?* to determine if you are aligned with your highest self.

and empathy, we can acknowledge and accept Joe as well. In this case, the action part of the Method is retraining our mind when tempted to judge with conscious thought.

Try this visualization to raise your perspective. Close your eyes and focus on a person in your life. Imagine you are on ground level, eye-to-eye. Feel what it is like to relate to that person on a one-on-one basis. Notice their frustrations, the joy, the way you interpret their behavior, and how you judge their character. Notice what you feel from this relationship.

Next, imagine stepping into a magical hot-air balloon. With each inhale you rise up into the sky, until you are floating above the trees. Each breath takes you closer to the clouds, each change of position offers a different perspective. You feel free, light, and one with nature. If you look upon that relationship from this perspective, what do you notice and how do you feel? If you could watch this person in their private time, what are their struggles, and what is the beauty you see in them in their quiet times? Whatever you see, can you gain more compassion, understanding, and allowance to welcome acceptance into your heart? From a new perspective can you understand how your actions or words might be affecting them in a way you didn't realize? Can you understand how much they try, or not, and allow their actions to teach you about their intentions?

Our minds are amazing tools, but if we process the world with limited perspective, it's not possible to fully engage our spiritual and emotional power. Keep in mind that each thought has an emotion attached to it. Even when your mind works to its fullest capacity, your emotional intlligence continues to ask for our attention.

As I write, I am very much in my mind. If I use conscious thought and recognize my feelings, I realize how excited I am to write and finish this book and share it with you. I have a sense of freedom in sharing my sleep story, and my hope is it will inspire freedom for you to share your truths. I also notice a twinge of insecurity, questioning if my work is enough or will the book make an impact? I feel desire in my heart to help others, and it feels so good. I notice fatigue. I am aware of all of these feelings as I write these words.

The emotions we have don't need to be "charged" in order to be noticed. They can be subtle, like an undercurrent of movement. The more we touch base with what we feel, the more we have a full experience of the truth in our current reality. It takes practice. An awareness of thoughts and feelings helps us to secure a spot in the present moment, overriding the toxic emotions from our past.

Some people think we shouldn't be too emotional, or let our emotions get the best of us. There's a difference in being emotionally attuned (intelligent) and emotionally out of control. From my personal experience, having an emotional fit on the streets in Manhattan isn't the preferred way to process. But emotional outbursts can (and do) happen. Optimally, the AAA Method provides the skills to recognize difficult emotions before they become volcanic.

Emotions are meant to flow, not become stagnant. If we stifle the movement of an emotion, we can become stuck. Trauma or other distressing life events have the potential to keep us stuck in the lowest vibrational emotion that relates to those events. While the mind attempts to protect us by deflecting from painful memories, that deflection is also halting healthy emotional processing.

Meditation has been shown to help those who suffer with PTSD because of the ability of the mind and emotions to be acknowledged and processed in a safe space. With practice, the inner world and higher consciousness learns to acknowledge thoughts, feelings, or triggers that arise. Instead of pushing them away by denial or distraction, meditation encourages us to be present and witness our thoughts and feelings in the moment. By allowing our thoughts and feelings to be present, we are better able to dissipate any threatening charge using the energy of acknowledgment and acceptance.

Pain and fear cause more pain and fear. Efforts to control or manipulate these difficult feelings hinder our ability to fully process them. We try to ward off anything that could potentially trigger a similar feeling in an effort to avoid more pain and fear, but this only creates a vicious cycle. If you've ever burned your finger and had a dramatic reaction to it, it's likely that you would develop pain or fear around stoves, fire, or potential threats. Whereas if you burned yourself and had a support system in place that was calm and attentive without inflating the "what if" fear factor, perhaps you would handle potential threats without as much pain or fear.

It makes sense that our mind would respond with pain or fear, but this reaction alone inhibits our ability to achieve a healing vibration. Love, forgiveness, and compassion are blocked when we focus on defending and denying fear, anger, resentment, and pain. Instead, allow the emotion of the event to be present and to process through so you can welcome new emotions that are connected with new experiences.

Love relationships are a breeding ground for negative emotional imprints. Negative reactions to a relationship that caused pain or fear can easily create expectations of more pain and fear in the next relationship, unless you focus on your own healing to rewrite your emotional imprint, raise your frequency, and meet someone at a new vibrational level.

Trust is fundamental to transforming toxic emotions. First, we must build self-esteem, gain confidence, and release any blame, shame, or guilt developed from our past so that we can trust ourselves. I encourage you to stay the course. Micro-shifts will snowball toward the development of new patterns to secure a safe place within. As you practice and shift, you may feel a rebirth of positive feelings and happiness, along with the ability to handle situations and relationships with a new energy. You may even feel as if your DNA changed, and hopefully that will be the case. Welcome the new growth, use your mind, and follow your heart to the highest and best sensation of aliveness!

Use this simple exercise when you are overthinking an issue or problem. For decisions that you find hard to make or concerns about a questionable relationship, ask yourself, *What do I feel?* Take a moment to step into conscious thought, connect into your emotional body, check the vibration, and see what you find. The mind can be tricky as it tries to rationalize and refer to old behaviors. By getting in touch with how you feel, you'll have a more accurate guide to alert you about the health and energy of a particular choice. Weigh each decision by pulling up the feeling of one option and checking the vibration, then pulling up the feeling of another option and checking the vibration, noticing any changes that feel like a higher, positive vibration or a lower, fearful one. Let the guide come from within you.

Mastering discernment helps to create stability and free old negative emotions such as resentment and judgment. Can you discern your feeling in the moment versus the thought about a feeling that you had in the past? Think of a negative memory, then remember what your belief or feeling was when you were experiencing that memory. Next, return to the present, and use the AAA Method to notice if your current feeling is different than the original. Do you still feel angry, sad, or bitter? Or are you attached to the original feeling and stuck in a belief pattern that you should still feel that way?

The brain processes thoughts, but take the time and space needed for your emotional body to activate so that you can process feelings. Otherwise you will continue to carry the same toxic emotions and expect different results. That isn't the path to good health.

Expanding the Heart

Expanding your heart and achieving stability are the final pieces to overcoming toxic emotions. Living with an open heart is essential to authenticity and healthy relationships. Not only will you feel the difference in your daily living, you may notice that your world becomes a softer and more enjoyable place.

We learn to close channels in our heart in order to lessen the risk of being hurt. If you've been hurt, you know the pain and fear that is associated with "putting your heart on the line" again. But self-love can help us feel safer and allow us to take risks to enter new relationships.

Experiencing love can be as scary as not being loved at all. At times it feels even more frightening. If we haven't felt worthy, lovable, or safe being intimate and vulnerable, we are going to experience similar feelings with the love we show ourselves. And it's common to place similar restrictions on relationships with others, whether we've realized it or not.

It takes daily practice to find stability in self-love and the ability to free a painful past. It won't come naturally if you haven't been given tools or seen healthy love in action. Be patient and gentle with yourself, but affirm your own growth by committing to using the AAA Method and showing up in each moment. Your inner child needs constant reassurance with attention, positive reinforcement, and encouragement, until they mature and feel stronger. Your inner child desires to be truly loved. Only you can satisfy this need.

Now that you better understand your patterns, your stories, and your truth, I hope you feel more confident to grow in love with yourself, being kind and gentle with yourself and with others. With changes to your emotional imprint, you will desire to experience the best for yourself and you will attract the same in return. This is the true form of manifestation—attracting that which resonates with your belief system and energetic frequency. To help continue on your journey, check out the exercises below. Review them when you feel stuck or when you are eager to rise up even further.

Heart-Opening Exercise: Put your right hand over your heart. Place your left hand over your right hand. Take three deep breaths. Bring to mind the sweet, innocent child that came into this world for a purpose. Feel compassion and hope in your heart as they learn and grow. Repeat this mantra out loud at least three times: "I deeply and completely love and accept myself."

Fire Ceremony: This ceremony should only be done in a safe and contained area with a firepit or fireplace. This exercise is most productive when there is a full moon, new moon, or seasonal solstice. Write down difficult thoughts or emotions from your past that linger in your mind or feel repetitive in relationships. Write a letter to your higher consciousness about the fear of letting go of old beliefs. Be honest and descriptive. Make sure that these words come from your heart. Write about your gratitude for self-care and love, for the opportunity to continue to change and grow. Fold the paper lengthwise or roll it into a cone shape. Light the bigger end while holding the paper in your other hand. Once the paper catches flame, put the rest of it into a flaming fire and as it burns, imagine the universe accepting your offering with gratitude, blessings, and love. Feel the lightness in your heart as you watch the last bits of these toxic emotions transform. With a humble spirit and a faith to surrender to the highest good, trust the divine energies to hear you and support your efforts in your world. You can now trust that what no longer serves the highest expression of you will be changed.

Exercise Your Heart: Movement is extremely helpful for the heart muscle, and the emotional muscle. Actively engage in yoga, aerobic exercise, Qigong, walking, rebounding, gentle running, or bicycling. Get the heart moving to allow new life energy to flow. In supporting our physical bodies, we support our emotional bodies as well.

Transformation happens daily. Change is the only constant, regardless of how much we want to tighten our grips on the past. When you make the choice to acknowledge change, acceptance of that change can bring opportunity along with the unknown. Take micro action steps to face difficult feelings and support your most innate desire to change. You have the power to spark the energy of transformation. You have the power to change your life, one moment at a time. Soon, you will dance to a new beat, with people who give you love and accept your love.

Our life journey is like a winding path. We spiral up and evolve toward a higher vibration, or we spiral down to be pulled back by the weight of our pain addictions. It is part of our life lesson to circle back to issues time and again. This is a normal part of the journey. Healing is a process. There is no quick fix. But when you feel weighed down by emotions, or thrown back into your old imprint by triggers, use the tools in this book to change the force of motion and move forward into higher consciousness. All of the answers are within you. At any moment you are only one thought, feeling, or action away from living a new life.

Self-Love Contract

This practice is to fully commit to your self-growth and self-love. Making a contract with yourself may seem silly, but putting pen to paper and signing your name can make a meaningful impact on your psyche and emotional imprint. Personal signatures are powerful. Your energy, personality, style, and uniqueness are displayed in your signature. This act is also one of respect to honor the work you've done and commit to do in the future. Live a life that is authentic, full, rewarding, and geared toward personal evolution that provides positive fuel to the world. Please write here or copy the following on a blank piece of paper and sign in ink.

Self-Love Contract

Date: _____

Location: _____

Name: _____

I, _____, hereby commit my best efforts to the growth and practice of self-love. I now recognize that I am worthy of my investment. Loving myself adds great value to my life and to the lives of others.

I, _____, am capable of learning new skills and techniques and I will apply them regularly to heal my inner child, build confidence in my adult self, and remember that self-love does not take away from my love for others, nor does it replace another's love for me.

I, _____, commit time each day to a mindfulness practice that is focused on the reality of my truth, and the expansion of my vibrational baseline. I am grateful for the stories of my past that shaped me, but they do not have to define me.

Loving myself,

Signature _____

Date _____

I hope this book and the AAA Method continue to serve your highest good so that you can vibrate higher, live happier, and have amazing relationships with yourself and others for all the years to come. There's nothing I love more than to help a person create positive change in their life using their own resources, determination, and spirit. Witnessing life being reborn as one rises up to meet their highest self is one of my greatest joys. I am very honored and humbled to be a part of your life and am grateful to have this opportunity to share my thoughts, stories, and truths. I trust that we will stay connected at some level for the rest of time.

Acknowledgments

WITH complete gratitude, I thank the Ones who arranged a meeting with John Willig; a fearless agent, a constant cheerleader, and a good friend without whom this book never would have happened. And to the publisher and editors, in particular Nicole Mele, who believed that this book was much needed in our world today, I am honored for your trust in me.

I'm indebted to my mother, Cheryl King, who in addition to my first book, has now spent even more hours editing this book. I imagine that wasn't part of her retirement plan, but I am so grateful.

Dear friends Helen Rodgers and Laura Zaccardi, who helped revise, edit, and comment with loving encouragement, I am very appreciative of your time, and for allowing me to be an absent friend while writing this book. And to Eve Salov, who has challenged me to look at deeper parts of myself, others, and life differently, I am grateful for your authenticity, humor, and love.

With equal gratitude I thank my father, Rick Guy, extended family members, and my many friends who continue to share their presence, wisdom, and love.

And for the one who inspires me most to keep going, even when life is arduous: Corkie, otherwise known as The Corkster, Corks, The Corkmeister, and Buddy. He is the epitome of overcoming adversity and a living example of pure love. To the outside world, it seemed he needed me in order to survive, but the reality is I needed him more.

Index

K
kindness, 36

L
laughter, 35
lies, 5
  to ourselves, 84
life, spiritual, 105
loneliness, 15, 22, 61–62
loss, xi
  acceptance and acknowledgment
    of, 136
love, xvi, 4, 36, 142. *See* Emotions
  as compassion, 133
  love letter to yourself, 114
  and pain, 133
  sending, 114
lymphatic issues, 22

M
Mad Money with Jim Cramer, 89
manipulation, 15
maturity, 24
meditation, 35, 138, 141
  practice, 55
  transcending-the-walls, 131–132
meme, 2
micro-steps, 9, 49–50, 95, 109, 137
mind, as line of defense, 136
mindfulness, 35, 53–54, 92, 95
money, 117
music, 35

N
narcissism, 37, 122
nature, connection to, 35
needs, meeting emotional, 102–105

options for, 104
  vs. relational needs, 102–103
needs, relational, 102–104
negativity, 16, 35
neglect, xvii, 3, 28
no, saying, xiv
nurturing, 18–19

O
obsession, sexual, 22
obsessive compulsive disorder, 22
outbursts, emotional, 22
overthinking exercise, 143
overwhelmed feeling, 15, 48–49,
  134
  AAA Method, 49–50, 134
ownership, 11

P
pain, xi, xv, xvi, 15
  addiction to, xvii, 30–31, 75, 125
  back, 22
  cycle of, xvii, 142
  and love, 133
parents, 19–20, 26–28, 31, 42–43,
  55, 99, 102, 126
  and blame, 20–21
  defending, 29–30
  ramifications of, 30
passion, 22
passivity, 22
past, acknowledging, 66
patterns, negative, xvi
peace, 36, 115
Peck, Scott, 5
people
  emotional type, 135

Notes

Notes

Notes

....
....
....
....
....
....
....
....
....
....
....
....
....
....
....
....
....

Notes

Notes

Notes

Notes

....

....

....

....

....

....

....

....

....

....

....

....

....

....

....

....

....

Notes

Notes

···

···

···

···

···

···

···

···

···

···

···

···

···

···

···

···

···

···

···

Notes

Notes

Notes

....
....
....
....
....
....
....
....
....
....
....
....
....
....
....
....
....
....
....